T4

HEROES' SQUARE
Budapest

András Gerő

HEROES' SQUARE
Budapest

HUNGARY'S HISTORY IN STONE AND BRONZE

*Photographs by
László Csigó*

Corvina

.

Translated by Christina Molinari
Translation revised by Chris Tennant

Design by Péter Maczó

© András Gerő, László Csigó

ISBN 963 13 2930 5
CO 2838-h-9092

Printed in Hungary, 1990
Kossuth Printing House, Budapest

The year was 1881. The Budapest General Assembly submitted a proposal to the National Assembly to build a monument commemorating the millennium of the conquest of Hungary. The monument was to record the events of a thousand years: appropriately commemorating the settlement of Hungary and the history of the Hungarian people. The proposal also represented much more. Eight years earlier the capital, formed from the three cities of Buda, Óbuda, and Pest, had been making its bid to become the true centre of the country. A great many of the city's inhabitants still spoke German, but the drive to assimilate to the Hungarian language and ways was well under way, providing all the more impetus for the development of a middle-class culture. These were the good old days of unprecedented drive toward modernization and the growth of a national consciousness—the main objectives of pre-First World War Budapest.

That same year the first centralized telephone network in the capital, the third anywhere in the world, was established, and the Hungarian News Agency was founded to ensure a modern network for the exchange of information. It was a period of consolidation and progress; of flourishing literary circles, theatres, coffee-houses, and taverns flooded with patrons; the time of a stable currency and a boom in industry, trade, and credit; an era when the government's party gained the majority in the national elections, and opposition parties spoke out but presented no particular threat; a period when the press was free. However carefree civilization seemed—and the conditions for life were relatively stable and secure—it could not be taken for granted that the problems that appeared to have been solved politically, had actually been solved.

With the Austro-Hungarian Compromise of 1867 *(Ausgleich)*, the Habsburg Empire had assumed its last form which, although established in a constitutional framework, still retained a good many absolutist laws. The Compromise accorded Hungary independence in domestic affairs and the right to preserve the territorial integrity of the entire country, including areas with mixed nationalities. However, all this was achieved at a great cost to the nation's absolute independence. The ministries of foreign affairs, national defense, and finance came under the empire's joint authority—a fact which had permanent damaging effect on national sentiment.

The political balance of power promoted acceptance of the status quo, but could do little to force the emotional identification of the people with the existing solution. Separate nationalities had no guaranteed collective rights under the dual monarchy, and in spite of the barrage of patriotic slogans, the system went far from pacifying the national sentiment of the majority of Hungarians, since it promoted modernization without complete national independence. Although things appeared to be running efficiently, many were actually waiting for the opportunity to change the situation in their favour. The threat of conflicting sentiments among nationalists and nationalities only served to intensify the social tensions concomitant with modernization. However secure Francis Joseph I, Austrian emperor and Hungarian king, might have felt of his position on the throne, the prospect of governing the empire was clouded by uncertainty.

Considering the state of affairs, the Millennial was not just an occasion for celebration: it was an opportunity. An opportunity for the government to construct an integrated national and historical ideology depicting the impaired statehood as though it were whole; presenting the status quo as the sole possibility open to the nation; and inspiring a sense of continuity—of permanent and unshakeable stability. But when would this opportunity be realized?

A great deal of controversy surrounded the issue of when the Magyars actually settled the area known as present-day Hungary. The Hungarian government, in 1882, solicited the help of the Academy of Sciences to determine the exact year of the Magyar Conquest. Scholars widely disagreed over the matter and after failing to reach a finally concluded consensus, reported: "All that can be stated with any certainty from the body of data we have examined is that the area known as modern Hungary had not been settled by the Magyars before A. D. 888 and that the occupation of the country was complete by 900—by that time the existence of the Hungarian state was certainly a fact." The Academy had designated a 12-year-time span when the Magyars may have settled the country, and it was left for the government to decide when the Millennial should actually be commemorated. After considerable deliberation, a statute was issued in 1892 setting the Millennial for 1895. Initially disregarding the capital's proposal, the government set about planning a large representative exhibition, later opting for a more extended project comprising a whole series of public construction works. Since time for implementing the plans was running out, the simplest recourse was inevitably to issue a statute in 1893, postponing the Millennial until 1896.

Meanwhile plans were beginning to shape up for the Millennial Celebration. Among the various ideas for the celebration, plans to establish a Millennial Monument were gaining ground. In February of 1894, a parliamentary document was drafted with prime ministerial approval, outlining the plans in greater detail. Several points of view emerged in the debate of the parliamentary committee established to look into the matter. The problem of where to locate the monument emerged as a key issue. One proposal favoured locating the statue of Árpád, founder of the nation, on Gellért Hill where the Citadel is today.

The problem of locating the monument merits special consideration, since the suggestion to erect it on Gellért Hill was not without its historical and political implications. The Citadel was built after the allied Austrian and Russian forces had crushed the Hungarian Revolution in 1849, which had threatened Habsburg rule by proclaiming an independent state. The building of the Citadel had been ordered by General Haynau, the hated and dreaded lieutenant-governor of Hungary, who had been invested with full authority over the land by young Francis Joseph. Having been completed in 1854, the Citadel was militarily obsolete, but then it had not actually been intended to provide effective military defence against possible armed attack. The Citadel's cannon were directed against Pest, site of the March Revolution of 1848, in order to intimidate the city's inhabitants. The Citadel came to symbolize oppression and was somewhat ironically referred to as the 'Bastille of Gellért Hill'. When the Compromise was established between the king and the nation in 1867, a suggestion was made to knock down the obsolete fortress, a disturbing reminder of Habsburg absolutism and quite out of accord with the tenuously established political accord.

The proposal to place the statue of the leader of the conquering Hungarian tribes, Prince Árpád, where the Citadel was had a clear political intent. The idea had surely been inspired by an earlier one conceived by Count István Széchenyi, considered "the greatest Hungarian", who had suggested building a pantheon on the hill where there was only a humble astronomical observatory. Instead of testifying to subjugation as the Citadel had, the statue would be built in its place to symbolize independence and glory.

The memorial was never built on the hill. Although the government weighed the merits of the proposal, high costs compelled it to table plans to knock down the Citadel and build another monument. A far less colourful solution was opted for: the Citadel was symbolically dismantled in 1897, with the part above the entrance destroyed and some of the walls disrupted. The fortress stayed where it was, although considerably divested of much of its original charm.

Instead of locating the projected triumphal arch on Gellért Hill, some maintained it should be built at the end of Andrássy Avenue, today Népköztársaság útja (the Avenue of the People's Republic), a

1. The end of Sugár út with the flag-post and the Gloriette designed by Miklós Ybl. 1880s

proposal which also won favour with the Prime Minister. For all practical purposes the issue was settled. Instead of being built on the site of the 'Bastille of Gellért Hill', the statue was to be located on Hungary's 'Champs-Élysées'. Once known as Sugár út (Radial Avenue) and subsequently named for Count Gyula Andrássy, the first prime minister after the Compromise, Andrássy Avenue represented Budapest's claim to status as a major metropolitan area. The multistory houses on the street, built during the mid-1880s, had been modelled after the Champs-Élysées in Paris where construction had by and large been completed in the 1850s and 60s. In order to make the resemblance complete, all that was needed was the triumphal arch. Plans for the Parisian Arc de Triomphe had been projected during the reign of Napoleon I, assuming its final form in 1836. Just as it had to the French, the Hungarian triumphal arch was to symbolize *grandeur et gloire*. Andrássy Avenue reflected the power of the growing middle class. The street was also the site of the first underground railway on the continent (the second in all of Europe), which was completed in time for the 1896 Millennial, and is still in operation. The importance attached to historical continuity is further exhibited in the fact that the first plans for the street had been suggested in 1841 by Lajos Kossuth, one of the outstanding figures of the reform movement. Although the street was not situated where he had originally proposed, it still reflected an

2. Entrance to the Millennial Exhibition. 1896

8

amalgam of national and middle-class interests.

At the end of Andrássy Avenue, where the monument was to be built, had originally stood the 'Gloriette', a terraced fountain, designed by the architect Miklós Ybl, which drew its waters from an artesian spring. Drilling for the fountain had been done by the engineer Vilmos Zsigmond in the 1860s and 70s, producing 74 degree centigrade water from a depth of 971 metres. This excellent spring supplied the water to the Széchenyi Baths in City Park, opened in 1913. The Gloriette was subsequently relocated in 1898 on today's Széchenyi Hill. The place where the artesian fountain had been on the square is now marked by a metal plate.

Now that plans and location for the statue had been decided upon the search began for a designer and the financial resources to cover expenses. Sculptor György Zala and architect Albert Schickedanz were commissioned to draft the plans. At that time, in 1894, Zala, 36 years old, could still be considered a relatively young artist. He had only been living in Budapest for 10 years, having studied beforehand in Vienna and Munich, as was fashionable among his peers. His first major commission had been the Honvéd Memorial on Dísz Square in the Castle District in 1893, which was dedicated to the memory of the Hungarian troops who had fought in the 1849 War of Independence and recaptured Buda from the Austrians. Devoid of exaggeration and dedicated to a subject of concern for the whole nation, the statue proved to be just the right letter of recommendation to the committee.

Schickedanz was 48 years old when he received the commission. He was a teacher at the Budapest School of Applied Arts, a clear indication he was a conservative artist, inclined to work in classical forms. He already collaborated with Zala, having designed the base of the Honvéd Memorial, but also had some prior experience in building monuments as well. He had been charged with designing the statue of Lajos Batthyány, first prime minister of Hungary, whom Haynau had commanded to be executed in 1849. He had also designed, in 1882, the base of the statue of Ferenc Deák on today's Roosevelt Square. The decision, therefore, as to whom to choose for designing the statue had fallen to artists who could be counted on to create a monument which would appeal to the aesthetic sensibility and conceptions of the committee, and who already had some prior experience in putting national values into concrete form. Zala and Schickedanz were eminently suited for the job of designing the largest historical monument in Hungary to date and particularly for investing it with the desired message.

Opposition to the monument centred on the fact that the group of statues in question would have a long-term impact on the cityscape; it would not only constitute the biggest but also the costliest of all monuments built to date. Whomever was awarded the commission would not only be assured of a place in history but also of a solid livelihood in the future. As the officially commissioned artists began work on the design, other sculptors and architects lobbied for an open competition to decide who would be honoured with the distinction of designing the monument. Designs for the monument having been finished quickly, the architectural branch of the Hungarian Engineering and Architectural Association con-

3–6. Designs made for the Millennial Monument

EZREDÉVES-EMLÉK

EZREDÉVES-EMLÉK

vened a 52-member plenum in November 1894. They objected to the Zala–Schickedanz plans primarily on aesthetic grounds. They felt that the monument would be out of place at the end of Andrássy Avenue and that, furthermore, it would be an eyesore and a public nuisance. Emphasizing responsibility to future generations, their findings only tended to throw more weight behind the open competition. Among the leaders of those opposed to the plans was Frigyes Schulek. His restoration of the Coronation Church, known as Matthias Church, had made his name a household word. (Not long after voicing his objections to the proposed monument he participated in the city beautification projected for the Millennial Celebration, providing the plans for the Fishermen's Bastion.)

The Prime Minister's opinion remained unswayed and Zala won the commission. A parliamentary committee was set up to examine the plans and duly proposed several changes. City Park at the end of Andrássy Avenue was still regarded as the best site for the monument. Moreover, the demands for the open competition were overridden on the grounds that the existing plans were sound and that time before the Millennial was quickly running out. The latter argument for rejecting the open competition had little factual basis, since there would have been more than enough time to build the monument. Furthermore, the gate to the National Exhibition—one of the main attractions at the Millennial Celebration—had been established on the spot where the monument was planned to go. And since the square could only accommodate one structure at a time, only after the exhibition had been taken down could building on the monument actually begin, a simple con-

sideration which had apparently occurred to no one before Zala signed the final contract in spring 1895. The contract stipulated that only the clay models for the statues would have to be ready by 1896, and that architectural work could begin in late 1896. The final date for completion was slated another five years after that. Some 800,000 forints had been earmarked for total costs, an astronomical sum and the largest amount of money which had ever been invested in any single work of art in Hungary. Indeed the government had spared no expense in this project. (To provide an idea of the value of the figures involved, the underground railway, one of the wonders of the contemporary world, had cost a total of 3.7 million forints.) How could the signers of the con-

7. *The equestrian statue of Árpád, leader of the Magyar tribes*

tract have known that it would not be five but nearly 35 years before the work would be finished, and that by the time the last bills were paid, neither the forint nor the korona, which later went into use, would be the official currency in Hungary.

By now the artists were busily working on implementing their plans. Zala reserved one of the storerooms at Western Railway Station, since it offered ample space for constructing the massive statues. The actual design, which only assumed its final form in 1929, was resolved rather ingeniously. The design for the triumphal arch projected an eclectic colonnade built in a double semi-circle; the colonnade would be 85 metres wide and 25 deep. The structure, facing the city, was planned to create the sense of an open triumphal arch. The base of the main group of statues stands a little forward at the centre of the colonnade, with Árpád, chieftain of the Magyar tribes and forebear of the nation's kings, assuming the foremost position. He is flanked by the equestrian statues of the other six tribal leaders. A 36-metre column emerges from the base capped by the bronze statue of the Archangel Gabriel—two times greater than the life-size human form—resting on a solid globe. In each hand he bears an important symbol—in one, the holy crown of the Hungarian kings and in the other, an apostolic cross. In the distance symbolic groups of bronze statues span the top of the colonnade. War is symbolized in the military chariot galloping on the left of the semi-circle, flanked by statues symbolizing Work and Welfare. On the right half of the semi-circle are the majestic chariot of Peace and the paired statues of Knowledge and Glory. In between the columns are the statues of the leading figures from Hungarian history sculpted in revival-

8. *The Archangel Gabriel*

ist style; beneath them are reliefs depicting scenes from the relevant periods of Hungarian history.

The symbols used in the monument—War, Peace, Work, Welfare, Knowledge, and Glory—are somewhat standard and could have been included in any country's national monument. The principal reason for including them in the work was the conventions they stand for. The symbol of the Archangel Gabriel has a more direct bearing on the nation's history. In addition to symbolizing victory, the holy crown and the apostolic cross lifted on high represent the triumph of Hungarian statehood as inseparable from Christian culture. The choice of Gabriel is also apt since, according to legend, the archangel appeared to the first Hungarian king in a dream, charging him to convert his people to Christianity.

Which statesmen would be represented in the monument and the grounds on which they were to be selected are issues in which contemporary views on and attitudes towards history clearly manifested themselves. There were 14 places to be filled. In the following pages, we shall present a history of the statues and reliefs, how they had been originally conceived and erected at various points in time, and how some of them came to be eventually replaced by others.

King Stephen (the Saint, 997–1038), the Hungarian prince who had converted the people to Christianity and, in accepting his crown from the Pope in 1001, had elevated Hungary to the status of kingdom and estab-

lished it as a state in accord with contemporary European norms—is the first statue represented in the proscenium. He is followed by the statue of King Ladislas (the Saint, 1077–95). In the relief below the statue, a noble act is depicted, his slaying of a Cumanian abductor. The choice of the theme, in addition to depicting the scene itself, revealed the intention of expressing national character. The enemy attacking the country was so evil that he did not desist from abducting defenceless women, until the Hungarian king forcefully intervened, thus postulating the notion of lawful and valiant self-defence. In short, Hungary's increase of power became justified through its noble intentions and lawful self-defence.

In another relief, King Coloman the

9. The symbolic statue of War

10. Work and Welfare

14

11. Knowledge and Glory

12. Peace

Beauclerc (1095–1116) is shown annexing Croatia and Dalmatia to Hungary, thus establishing the nation's territorial claim. The next scene again emphasizes Hungary's inseparability from Europe: the participation of King Andrew II in medieval Europe's largest collective enterprise, the Crusades, symbolizing the active defence of Christian faith and devotion. The next relief depicts the Mongol Invasion of 1241–42, which dealt a devastating blow to the country. King Béla IV (1235–70) is shown rebuilding the medieval Hungarian state from the ruins of the invasion, embodying the ideal of unceasing, heroic activity and the spirit of reconstruction.

The subsequent statue-relief pair, one of the most unusual elements of the monu-

ment, represents Charles Robert (1308–42), descended from the Angevin House, who greatly contributed to organizing the economic-political structure of the state. In the face of internal dissention and incursions by powers such as the Habsburgs, Charles Robert successfully defended the nation. In contrast to the statue, the relief below depicts an unrelated scene—the Battle of Marchfeld on August 26, 1278 where the Hungarian king, Ladislas IV (the Cuman, 1270–90), hastened to the assistance of Rudolph Habsburg. The allies proceeded to defeat the Czech king, Ottocar, who had encroached upon their power (and subsequently died in battle). Rudolph had this victory to thank for the valuable acquisition of the Austrian princedom, later proving

15

vital to the Habsburg dynasty. The content of the relief is striking not only because it is at variance with the statue above, but since it was meant to convey a given political message. Charles Robert was of incomparably greater historical significance as a ruler than Ladislas IV, and his presence in the monument suggests he was included out of respect for his historical importance, while the relief below is meant to convey the fact that it was the Hungarian people whom the Habsburgs had to thank for their position of power in Austria. No less noteworthy is the fact that when the monument was constructed a Habsburg ruled the country which constituted one half of the Empire. The reference to the Battle of Marchfeld was also meant to show that acceptance of the common fate provided the sole guarantee of protection against the Slavs and other would-be conquerors. Interdependence, loyalty, and national pride and consciousness were the ideological factors which had figured prominently in the 1867 Compromise. Depiction of the Battle of Marchfeld—otherwise so incongruent with the rest of the monument—was an especially good choice for demonstrating the historical viability of Hungarian nationalism within the empire.

Historically, Habsburg domination was still a long way off; the next three statues depict figures representing periods of national greatness preceding the Habsburg rule.

The reign of Louis I the Great (1342–82) saw the greatest expansion of territory in the nation's history. The relief focuses on the event when the king marched into Naples in 1348, received by Johanna who ruled here. (Louis was later forced to relinquish possession of Naples, for which he was given some financial compensation.)

The next statue represents the only non-royal personage in the monument, János Hunyadi (b. 1407?–56), who although only acted as governor of Hungary, held the actual power. The event recorded on the relief is one of world-wide importance. In 1456 at Belgrade Hunyadi's forces forestalled the Turkish onslaught, ensuring the country's own defence as well as that of all Europe. The relief shows a scene in which a Turkish soldier, who had attempted to hoist the Turkish flag on top of the wall of the besieged fort, is seized by a Hungarian soldier, the two of them plummeting together to their death. Including the Battle of Belgrade as part of the monument was meant to demonstrate that Hungary had not simply defended its own territorial integrity, but had offered itself up in selfless defence of Europe and European civilization.

The final figure represented in this series is the great Renaissance ruler of Hungary, Matthias Hunyadi (Corvinus, 1458–90), who took up the rule from his governing father. Renowned for his humanistic learning and enlightened court Matthias is depicted in the relief surrounded by his scholars. By emphasizing Matthias's role as a great patron of arts and sciences, the magnitude of the nation's cultural contribution was also exposed.

The statue and relief of Matthias is followed by the representation of the Habsburg dynasty. The Habsburgs had held continuous power over Hungary since the reign of Ferdinand I (1526–64), although Ferdinand himself was unable to defend the country from the Turks and in fact divided forces in his struggle to secure power. Once again the relief below is at variance with the

13. Habsburgs on the Millennial Monument: Ferdinand I, Charles III and Maria Theresa

statue. The scene depicted is the valiant and victorious battle at Eger Castle in 1552, when the Hungarian soldiers successfully put down a Turkish siege. The battle is legendary for the role women played in the struggle, picking up weapons beside their male counterparts, and they are shown in the relief fighting alongside the men. The inclusion of the relief under the statue of a Habsburg ruler expresses no little ambivalence over the fact that Hungary had to resort to waging its own battles in the interest of self-preservation.

The same contrast between the message in relief and statue is evidenced with respect to the statue of Charles III (1711–40). The relief beneath his statue depicts the decisive victory against Turkish forces under Eugene of Savoy at Zenta in 1697, marking the end of some 150 years of Turkish occupation. However, the ruler during this era was Leopold I (1657–1705), whom the Hungarians had rebelled against, first under Thököly's leadership and later under Ferenc Rákóczi II. To depict the very king who had flagrantly disregarded national rights and dealt with Hungary as though it were a mere subjugated province would have gone far to risk popular resentment. If Rákóczi, who had fought so hard for state independence, had himself been excluded from those represented in the monument, then no statue of Leopold would be included either. Represented in the monument instead was Charles III who, after the struggle for freedom led by Rákóczi, was able to implement the compromise which had brought fighting to an end. Charles III replaces Leopold as the ruler who had been responsible for seeing through the Austro–Hungarian agreement.

The inclusion of the statue of Maria Theresa (1740–80) reflects the view that if a ruler acted in accord with Hungarian law Hungary would be quick in rendering assistance. The relief below the queen's statue depicts the scene in which the Diet voted in 1741 in Pozsony to send her military support with the exclamation, *"Vitam et sanguinem!"* If Hungary had refused assistance to the ruler at that crucial point in history, the Habsburg Empire would certainly have been annihilated, since Maria Theresa's right to the throne was not recognized abroad and the Prussians and Bavarians had launched an attack against her country. Hungarian soldiers had halted their campaign, a fact which had not only made possible the reoccupation of Austria and Bohemia, but had also won diplomatic recognition of Maria Theresa's sovereignty. The relief refers to two historical events in which Hungary had proven itself to be a reliable buttress for the Monarchy: the aiding of the Habsburgs to power in the 13th century and the saving of the Empire from total collapse in the 18th century. It is therefore only befitting that they should receive help from a just ruler, in the event that their rights are violated; for this reason the statue of Leopold II is included among the others. Here again we have an example of a situation in which the artistic work is subordinated to political interests. Whereas Maria Theresa's prominence in history was indisputable, Leopold II had actually ruled for less than two years (1790–92). The sole and exclusive reason for his inclusion in the

monument was that he at least recognized, if in name only, the Hungarian feudal constitution which had been ignored by his predecessor, the son of Maria Theresa, Joseph II (1780–90). To avoid having to give account of his acts as king to the Diet, Joseph II had not permitted himself to be crowned and had sent the Holy Crown to Vienna. Leopold II's reign saw the restoration of the crown to Buda. This is the scene depicted on the relief, reflecting the restoration of relations between the Habsburgs and Hungary, viz. provided that certain rules of the game are adhered to, the Hungarian–Habsburg relations would ensure the preservation of national interests. At the same time, the message of the relief indicated that the nation, in defence of its legal integrity, was capable of evoking honourable and successful resistance to Joseph II, who had ignored its constitution.

The last statue is that of Francis Joseph (1848–1916), the reigning monarch, shown in full military dress. Everything concerning the Habsburgs in the monument thus far had been presented in such a way as to depict his world as one of perfected harmony. The relief below it shows the crowning of Francis Joseph in 1867 by the Hungarian prime minister Gyula Andrássy and the head of the nation's Catholic church.

14. The relief under the statue of Francis Joseph showing his coronation

The scene is also remarkable for its depiction of the graceful figure of Queen Elizabeth, much beloved by the Hungarian people, and the presence of Ferenc Deák, the leading figure behind the Austro–Hungarian Compromise. With the coronation of Francis Joseph the long-awaited peace between king and country had been established, and Hungary had at last settled into its role in the empire, a place it had duly accepted in the spirit of the Compromise which—as had been the firm belief of its framers—would ensure the territorial integrity of the state, promote the development of the Hungarian nation, and designate a political field for the play of national sentiment and aspiration. Only through allegiance to both Monarchy and country—contemporaries believed—would true unity emerge.

It is true that in the eyes of contemporaries, this sense of harmony must have been disturbed by the figure of a monarch in full military garb. It served as a reminder that the defeat of the 1848–49 War of Independence and the ensuing terror of absolutism were also embodied in the same person. Although those days might safely be regarded as over, the somewhat disturbing thought remained that it was the ruler who was invested with exclusive power to summon the armed forces under the re-established constitution. In short, suppose that this were not the best of all possible worlds, it was necessary to create a new view of history immersing the present in past glory and giving an impression of unfailing continuity and fulfilment. Summing up the message that the Millennial Monument had set out to convey, we find a unique fusion of national character and politics embedded in a unique history. It showed the Hun-

garians as great fighters, chivalrous, self-assured and capable of great undertakings. They struggled heroically for themselves and others, were prepared to make sacrifices in defending their rights, and were open to European culture. As long as kings were willing to respect the customs and laws, they would be accorded the unbounded loyalty of the Hungarian nation. Hungary's embracing of Christianity was not simply an expression of its becoming a European state but reflected a commitment to defend Christian values and to fight for them when necessary. The place the Hungarian state had assumed within the Habsburg Empire was not only regarded as an accepted possibility but, moreover, the only one.

However great the initial surge of activity had been, work on constructing the monument had been quite slow, and extended so far beyond the allotted time that it had failed to keep pace with political changes which emerged. Realizing that he would not be able to finish work on the statues himself by the appointed time, Zala commissioned six other sculptors to work on some of the other sculptures. He then set about the task of carving the Archangel Gabriel, which was ready by June 1897. The end of the year saw the colonnade established in place, and it looked as though work on the Millennial Monument would be completed by the appointed deadline.

Due perhaps to lingering hostility over the scrapping of the open competition, the Bureau of Engineers began to find fault with the construction. Insisting that the archangel would be swept from the 36-metre column in the first serious storm, they consented to putting up the statue only when an iron rod had been secured within the column. This entailed building an entirely

15. The statue of the Archangel Gabriel in the Art Gallery

were finished, with the statue of Matthias Hunyadi (by György Zala) cast in 1905, along with those of Ferdinand I (by Ede Margó), Béla IV (Miklós Köllő), Charles Robert (György Kiss), and Leopold II (Richárd Füredi). Work was then completed on the twin statues of Work and Welfare, as well as Knowledge and Glory.

Statues finished by 1906 included those of King Coloman the Beauclerc (by Richárd Füredi), János Hunyadi (Ede Margó), and the Chariot of War (György Zala). Zala completed the statues of Francis Joseph and the symbolic figure of Peace by 1908. As statues went up with regularity, the colonnade slowly began to assume its final form. The year 1911 saw the casting of the statues of Saint Ladislas (by Ede Telcs), Saint Stephen (by Károly Senyei), and Maria Theresa (by György Zala). That same year five of the completed reliefs joined the monument which by this time was becoming the capital's newest landmark. To the existing statues were added, in 1912, the statues of Andrew II (by Károly Senyei), Charles III (by Ede Telcs), as well as the equestrian statue of Árpád (by György Zala).

With the statues of a king and six leaders as well as some five reliefs remaining, plans to complete the monument were interrupted by the First World War. The nation's involvement in the war demanded the channelling of its energies into military areas. Official propaganda was already overemphasizing the themes of national greatness and glory. As long as these were borne out by victory, they were effective. Later, as the war grew more protracted and military victories fewer, people became increasingly more conscious of what the nation's leaders had known from the outset,

new column which was finished by the fall of 1901. Meanwhile the bronze statue of Gabriel was sent to Paris for the 1900 World Exhibition. It received the Grand Prix. Many even at that time had rightly realized that the statue's location high above the monument would not do justice to the fine sculptural details. At a distance of over seven stories the beauty of the statue is indeed lost to the observer's eye. The statue of Gabriel has occupied this remote place at the top of the column since the autumn of 1910.

Although the colonnade and Gabriel were up, the monument was far from being complete without the statues, which were long in preparation. The National Council of Fine Arts received the works in the order they i.e. Hungary could only emerge as a loser from the war. Had the Monarchy, fighting on the German side, proven victorious, it would have increased its territory, but not that of Hungary, because apart from the *Csángó,* a Hungarian ethnic group living in the Rumanian Kingdom, all Hungarians were living within the national boundaries of Hungary. Also, during the peaceful decades under the Dual Monarchy, the other nationalities had been assimilated as well. The 1910 census showed a Hungarian majority. The territorial expansion implied by a Habsburg victory, however, would have increased the proportion of Slavic peoples, thus jeopardizing the political leadership of Hungarians within the country and also endangering the balance of power within the Dual Monarchy. Nevertheless losing the war would prove to have even greater unforseeable consequences, bringing with it the threat of disintegration of a multinational country. So, solely for the sake of maintaining the status quo, a tremendous loss of life was incurred.

No national interests could justify the loss of thousands of Hungarian soldiers and countless others—the soil of Galicia and Italy was piled with row upon row of Hungarians who had died so far from their homeland. Meanwhile the standard of living in the country had plunged, the supply of goods and foodstuffs to the people having been syphoned off by the war machine. What had been originally feared came about: the Monarchy had lost the

16. The statues of the Habsburg monarchs dismounted during the 1919 Republic of Councils

war. Minorities living within Hungary saw their opportunity to break free, an event the consequences of which were impossible to assess until after the war had actually ended in 1918. In any event the prediction made by the critics of the 1867 Compromise was fulfilled. Hungary, as part of the Habsburg Empire, was incapable of preserving its territorial integrity, since it failed to offer acceptable compromises to its minorities at the relevant time.

The loss of the war, combined with social tensions in Hungary during the post-war period, created a revolutionary climate. The revolution in October 1918 ushered in promises of democratic rights and land reform. A republic was declared. It is understandable that the country, suddenly gaining its independence, even though its boundaries had yet to be drawn, sought to define itself in contrast to the Habsburg Monarchy. They were convinced that this was the only way to recoup its losses.

Attempts were made to re-interpret the nation's history, bringing into focus those events—primarily those of 1848—reflecting anti-Habsburg sentiments. Indicative to the prevailing atmosphere of the times was the fact that Joseph Habsburg, the king's representative, had proposed changing his last name to Alcsút, the name of the place where he held estates. Also characteristic of this period was the radical direction that events took in the social and political spheres as the proletariat assumed power in March, 1919. While the problem of the

17. The broken statue of Francis Joseph

18. The Millennial Monument decorated for the May Day Parade in 1919

nation's future officially became of secondary importance (if the world revolution were victorious, the issue of national boundaries was believed to lose its relevance), the Habsburgs were invested with a new image seen from the perspective of feudalist–capitalist oppression. Statues of members of the Habsburg dynasty were duly eliminated from the monument, and the statue of Francis Joseph—directly associated with the regime that had been in power during the war—was smashed to pieces.

The revolution was short-lived and the victory of the counter-revolution saw the reinstitution of the kingdom, deriving its legitimacy from the Hungary existing during the Dual Monarchy. This was necessary not only for reasons of internal legitimacy but for foreign policy as well. By 1920, external constraints imposed as a result of Hungary's loss of the war, were more clearly defined in the Treaty of Trianon forced upon Hungary during the course of the Paris peace negotiations. Signing the peace had been a precondition for international recognition of the counter-revolutionary regime. Paradoxically, the government which owed its very existence to the signing of this treaty, proceeded to aim its entire policy at eradicating the status quo established by the terms of that treaty.

Under the terms of the dictated peace agreement new borders were drawn. Hungary lost 191,735 square kilometres of territory from the original 282,870, and was left with a somewhat smaller area than had been accorded to Rumania alone. Eleven million of its population of 18,000,000 found themselves in the status of minorities in neighbouring states. Particularly difficult to accept was the fact that the ethnic considerations had not been taken into account in drawing up the new borders; moreover, no national plebiscite had been called as pledged by the victorious powers of the Entente. Thus, over three and a half million Hungarians were suddenly subject to foreign jurisdiction. War, revolutions, the severe economic terms of the peace agreement, and Hungarians relocating from other countries contributed to exacerbate the situation. The country was plunged into a state of economic emergency. Added to this was the fact that hundreds of thousands of families were mourning war victims. The terms dictated by the Treaty of Trianon left the country in a defenceless and vulnerable position *vis-à-vis* its neighbours whose territories had increased. For every Hungarian soldier, there were five Czech, six Rumanian, and four Yugoslavian.

The disintegration of historical Hungary, understandably enough, left the people in a state of shock. The fact that so much had been lost at the mercy of grossly unjust terms of peace shook the nation's sense of justice. Hungarian nationalist sentiment would have found it difficult enough to resign itself to the more or less unavoidable disintegration of historical borders, but the way in which it came about proved to be intolerable. Neither bourgeois democratic revolution nor proletarian class solidarity had been able to forestall the tragedy; the revolutions that had failed for a variety of reasons only served to reinforce adherence to conservative principles. The counter-revolutionary regime associated the ex-

clusive cause of the nation's problems with the manifest outcome. The inability of other political forces to prevent the tragedy gave the government all the more reason for the shift in ideology. The regime used historical claims as an ideo-political counter-balance to the national tragedy, asserting that the loss of national territory had been a direct consequence of national independence and that the Monarchy had proved the only enduring political framework. The liberal policies of the Austro–Hungarian Monarchy had led to the emergence of 'destructive' revolutionary forces. Thus, the Hungary of the Dual Monarchy became mythicized, and anti–liberalism set in.

In the new political climate, the Habsburgs resumed their place of honour. The statues were returned to their places, and the statue of Francis Joseph recast, having been so severely damaged during the revolution. This time the king was no longer in full military regalia, but clothed in the coronation robes. By dressing the king in majestic robes, the regime hoped to emphasize its historical claims while rebuffing the framers of the Treaty of Trianon. In the interests of avoiding re-establishment of the old state configuration, it had been decreed that no Hungarian king could be descended from the Habsburg line. Paradoxically, a good many members of the Hungarian National Assembly wept while casting their vote in 1921 for the abolition of the Habsburg line. The coronation mantle thus devolved into a kind of local, political symbol of resistance and obstinate faith.

Although the statues of the Habsburgs were returned to the monument, the work as a whole was still unfinished. Schickedanz had died, and in 1921 György Zala sent a memorandum to Nicholas Horthy, Regent

19. The Millennial Monument in the 1920s

of Hungary, governor of a kingdom now divested of its king. The memorandum requested a fresh sum of money to complete work on the monument. By now all the country's financial resources were tied down by post-war reconstruction; while the new regime would have readily appropriated the patriotic symbols in the monument for its own, the tight national budget would not allow the expense. Consequently, Zala and his monument had to wait.

At the beginning of this same year a proposal was made which, although of an apparently different nature, would later have a direct impact on the Millennial Monument. The National Association of Hungarian War Veterans proposed that a large-scale memorial be raised to comme-

morate the heroism of Hungarians during the war and the great sacrifice made on the part of Hungarian soldiers. The suggestion won overwhelming support, and by late 1922 an entire movement was under way to back the proposal, with the Minister of Education Count Klebelsberg giving final approval for the establishment of the monument. However, the decision was not put into action. It was not until March 16, 1924 that the National Council of Fine Arts announced a competition to choose the designer of the National Heroes' Memorial. Submissions were to remain anonymous until after the selection of the winning design.

Competitors had only a short time to submit their applications by the May 1

25

deadline. The first prize was one million crowns, second prize half that amount (which by the standards of the colossal inflation of the day would have meant about three pounds sterling to the first place winner, and one and a half pounds to the second). In addition to the design, applications had to specify the future location of the work and its method of construction. Stiff competition rules, narrow deadline, and unattractive prize notwithstanding, the judge's committee received some 190 submissions.

Having received the permission and allocations necessary for finishing the Millennial Monument, Zala was back to work by 1926, completing the remaining five reliefs that same year.

21. Kond

20. The Magyar tribal leaders Ond and Tétény

Meanwhile the idea was raised that, by way of protesting the political consequences of the lost war, a memorial to those who had fallen in the war should be erected. Although many imaginative ideas were put forward, in the interests of expediency the final choice went to a simple slab to be placed at the base of the Árpád statue in the Millennial Monument.

Now that the work had been sanctioned by the powers-to-be, by 1928 all the necessary conditions had been established for finishing the Millennial Monument. Zala worked furiously on the project, and in 1928 the equestrian statues of the Magyar tribal leaders Előd, Ond, Kond, and Tas were duly set up alongside that of Árpád. With the consent of Horthy, Prime Minis-

22. Árpád

a coarsely worked tombstone. The monolith was surrounded by a stone parapet, inside which was a grassy area with a step leading up to it. The front side was inscribed with the dates 1914–1918, and the back with the words: "Dedicated to the 1000-year-old national borders." In addition, the top was engraved with a cross in the shape of a sword-hilt.

It was finally decided that, instead of being dedicated to the unknown soldier, the memorial placed alongside the fierce warriors of the Magyar Conquest was to pay homage to heroes, and even then not in the abstract sense of heroic valour, but within the context of one particular event, i.e. the First World War, an event which had exerted such a decisive influence on the nation's

23. Előd

ter István Bethlen set the dedication day of the National Memorial for May 26, 1929, which carried with it the implication that the entire monument would have to be ready by then as well. Zala rushed work on the equestrian statues of chieftains Huba and Töhötöm (Tétény). All the statues now in place, the effect was one of cold sobriety conveyed through a dreary eclecticism.

Work on the Memorial also had to be rushed, since the stone slab and not the monument had been officially scheduled for dedication. Owing to its massive proportions, the block of limestone weighing 47 metric tons, had to be transported to the square by special means. Measuring 6.5 metres long, 3 metres wide, and 1.3 metres high the monument gave the impression of

24. Huba

But by the time the monument had been finished the Monarchy had collapsed, and with it the historical boundaries of Hungary. The conservative counter-revolutionary regime did not learn from these events that their former image of historical greatness had been a deceptive one; instead they exclusively emphasized the injustice of the Treaty of Trianon and set as their unrealistic goal the restoration of the former boundaries. And while the original monument had been established to honour the present, by 1929 the monument had become the expression of the nation's goals for the future as willed by the existing regime.

By 1929 the monument had become an inseparable part of the capital and a national landmark. The site of the monument at the

25. Tas

history. The true hero fought to maintain the borders which had been in existence for 1000 years and to re-establish those borders when they had been lost. Ironically, the memorial was thus dedicated to the soldiers of that very same war in which they had lost everything they had been fighting for.

With the inclusion of the memorial in the Millennial Monument the original message of the monument was to some extent modified. The original intent in designing the monument had been to convey a kind of self-complacent patriotism—to assert that Hungary had achieved its manifest destiny within the framework of the Dual Monarchy and that the assumption of this role marked the culmination of its natural historic path of 1000 years of development.

end of Andrássy Avenue was named Heroes' Square in 1932, in line with the shift in the original meaning. During 1937–38 the square was paved with flagstone for the Eucharistic Congress. Trees, flowers, and the fountains on either side were removed. The square lost much of its original charm and intimacy, becoming stern and imposing.

After thirty years of work of varying intensity on the monument operations had appeared to have reached a standstill; however, this was not to be the case. Sixteen years later individual statues and reliefs were once again removed to make way for new ones.

In 1945 the nation lost another world war. The regime's political aims during the 1930s to restore the former boundaries had drawn Hungary into alliance with Nazi Germany, which also sought to do away with the Treaty of Paris. Hungary initially benefited from the alliance, reclaiming disannexed territories in succession—formerly Northern Hungary and Ruthenia from Czechoslovakia in 1938 and 1939, a section of Transylvania from Rumania in 1940, and its former southern part from Yugoslavia in 1941. Nevertheless greater military involvement was also incumbent upon the alliance with Germany; Hungarian troops were soon at war with the Soviet Union, and war had been declared against the U.S. and Great Britain. By this time, policies had ceased to serve national interests, and had become increasingly fascist as a result of

26. Heroes' Square at the time of the Eucharistic Congress in 1938

27. *The war is over*

28. *Washing-day on Heroes' Square in May, 1945*

Hungary's alliance with Germany. Thus in 1945 the nation once again found itself on the losing side; the fascist machine had plunged Hungarian soldiers and countless other innocent people into senseless annihilation.

With the arrival of the Soviet troops, a new leadership was established where all antifascist forces were represented, including the Communist Party which had formerly been banned. The new political order rallied under democracy, and new democratic principles emerged. The political forces which had swept the country into war were as much anathema to the new regime as their outmoded political slogans, and the new government sought to proclaim new ideals. To safeguard the nation's future

Hungary had to be kept democratic and independent, established in peaceful coexistence with its neighbours. The concept of an independent, democratic, popularly-backed state was out of keeping with the symbolism originally inherent in the monument, and political forces once again set about to impose a new image and values upon it.

The Habsburg statues—two of which suffered extensive damage during the war—were taken out again in 1945 and exchanged for historical figures who were more in keeping with national independence: Ferdinand I was replaced by István Bocskai who had led a successful uprising against the Habsburg dynasty at the beginning of the seventeenth century and had been chosen by the estates as ruling prince (1605-6). Since the statue of Bocskai by Barnabás Holló had once been on what is today known as Kodály körönd, it was simply moved to a new location at the end of Andrássy Avenue. All the reliefs depicting scenes from the Habsburg dynasty were also removed. The relief under Bocskai's statue by László Martin depicted a military scene, showing his soldiers fighting imperial mercenaries.

Charles III's statue was replaced by that of Gábor Bethlen, Prince of Transylvania (1613–29) who, in the face of the disintegrating Hungarian state at war with the Turks and the Habsburg emperor, perpetuated national culture and statehood by attempting to reunify Hungary through building a strong Transylvania. While waging successful struggles against the Habsburgs, he had made an ill-fated alliance with the Czech estates who were quickly beaten by the emperor. The relief by István Szabó, emphasizing the scene from Bethlen's colourful biography where he is entering into the agreement with the Czechs constitutes a good-will gesture on the part of the new political order toward the Czechs: such an act had its political implication in 1945, the year when Hungarians were being forcibly relocated from Czechoslovakia. Despite the new political order in Czechoslovakia, the principle of collective retribution had been exercised against Hungarian nationals. Bethlen's statue was likewise moved from Kodály körönd to the Millennial Monument.

29. Mass meeting on Heroes' Square on May Day, 1945

The statue of Maria Theresa was exchanged for that of Imre Thököly, renowned for his role as leader of an anti-Habsburg movement during the 1670s and 80s. The relief, by Jenő Graetner, depicts a scene from his short-lived success, the battle of Szikszó fought on 3 November 1679. Bocskai's soldiers, the *Hajdús* and Thököly's *Kuruts,* both represented in the monument, each symbolize military success in the struggle for national independence. Despite the massive defeat in the Second World War, the monument served to reinforce the belief that the nation had been capable of military success and demonstrating military prowess where real national interests were at stake.

The statue of Leopold II was replaced by that of Ferenc Rákóczi II, Prince of Transylvania (1704–11). The leader of the largest Hungarian anti-Habsburg movement prior to the nineteenth century had waged enormously successful struggles in the period between 1703 and 1711. Without the support of the peasants, who had pinned high hopes on victory from the very start, the success of the movement would have been inconceivable. The relief depicts Rákóczi's return home from Poland to the welcome of the serf army in 1703 under Tamás Esze, who had risen from peasant origins to assume command of the Hungarian insurgents.

Francis Joseph's statue was replaced by that of Lajos Kossuth. Referred to by the Hungarian people as "Father Kossuth", the leader of the 1848–49 War of Independence has indeed become a part of Hungarian national mythology. His name became equated with national independence, not only because he proposed, at the National Assembly in 1849, that the Habsburgs be de-

throned, but also because he remained committed to the cause of the country's independence right to the end, until he died in emigration. The peasantry held him in great esteem as well, because they associated the abolition of serfdom with his name. The relief, in fact, shows him summoning the peasants of the Great Plain to arms. The statues of Rákóczi and Kossuth are both the work of Zsigmond Kisfaludi Strobl. In the representation of these two leading historical figures it was the peasantry who had figured most prominently—now regarded by statesmen as one of the mainstays of democratic Hungary and largely responsible for its national glory and success.

The monument continued to undergo changes in form and thus in meaning. The National Heroes' Memorial was removed in accordance with the new anti-revisionist policy. Also a relief depicting territorial expansion—the scene originally below King Coloman the Beauclerc's statue dealing with the theme of the annexation of Croatia and Dalmatia—was removed. It was replaced by a relief recording another action of the ruler, the prohibition of the burning of witches. The relief was in praise of his enlightened thought, but omitted the historical fact that the king had not prohibited *all* witchcraft, only the *strigas,* witches who had the power to change into animals, were to be spared from the death penalty. In the interests of establishing friendly relations with Czechoslovakia, the relief beneath Charles Robert's statue depicting the Habsburg–Hungarian alliance against the Czechs at the 1278 Battle of Marchfeld was also slated to be removed, but, perhaps for financial reasons, only the inscription below the relief was eliminated.

With the new changes in the monument

the political message had slightly altered. While upholding the value of medieval *grandeur et gloire* imbued with Christianity, the emphasis on continuity shifted to national independence, and in the upward-spiralling history of the nation in its advance toward development, an ever greater role was ascribed to the people. Real importance was attached not to the nation's borders, but to the political order existing within. This way the new political system that came to power after 1945 stated its own goal as well, that of building an independent and democratic new Hungary, while preserving valuable parts of its traditions.

Under the advance of Stalinism the values embodied in the monument in 1945 received only formal recognition. During this period, the concept of independence had become an empty slogan, while a similar fate had befallen democracy. Historical continuity was sought for in other traditions. The regime ascribed particular importance to peasant uprisings and class struggles in general, to those traditions which could be reformulated along revolutionary lines. This period was also characterized by anti-religious sentiment which took institutionalized, as well as ideological, opposition against Christianity. The current regime stood in direct opposition to the symbolism of kingship and Hungary's Christian allegiance to Europe which had been employed in the monument.

Obviously they would have gladly wiped the monument, with all its archangel and kings off the face of the earth. However, they were unable to do so, for two reasons. First of all, many of the figures represented in the monument had already been appropriated by the regime for its own use. And secondly, the regime which had regarded itself as the implementor of reforms begun in 1945 could not do away with the monument that they had a share in transforming. Nevertheless, no attempt was made to build a new Heroes' Memorial. While the removal of the first Memorial was viewed as being in line with post-war reform, the existing leadership did not erect a new one in its place, because they regarded the Hungarian people as guilty for having stood by Hitler to the end of the war. Building another Memorial to the Unknown Soldier on the square would have been tantamount to honouring the Hungarian army which had fought on the side of the fascists. Nevertheless, during the summer of 1956, in the political climate following the death of Stalin, the National Heroes' Memorial by Béla Gebhardt was returned to the site of the monument, this time inscribed to the memory of those who had given their lives for the freedom of the Hungarian people. With this event the molding of the monument to the new conceptual framework introduced in 1945 essentially comes to an end.

The Millennial Monument has retained its present shape since 1956 and the earlier process of transformation appears to have come to a halt. By the very nature of the political and historical messages the monument set out to convey it constitutes all of Hungarian history condensed to a single symbol. This symbol was constantly altered and transformed by changes in Hungarian history—prevailing political views shaped it in their own likeness. The history of the monument is reflective of the period in which it was created. In spite of its solid form it underwent perpetual change along with the major turning-points in the nation's history, and its changes mirror the historical changes which took place.

Leaving behind the story of the monument's creation, let us now turn our attention to the figures themselves and the history lying behind them.

As we approach Heroes' Square from Népköztársaság Avenue, the entire impression is one of symmetricality. On the right is the Art Gallery, designed in eclectic style by Albert Schickedanz and Fülöp Herzog for the 1896 Millennial; it is the largest exhibition hall in the capital and host to many temporary exhibitions. Badly damaged during the Second World War, work on restoring the gallery was completed in 1950. Also built in eclectic style on the left of the square is the Museum of Fine Arts. Although more massive in proportion than the Art Gallery, it does not disturb the symmetricality of the square. Also designed by Schickedanz and Herzog, it was officially opened on December 1, 1906. The Museum of Fine Arts contains what is, by any standard, the most significant Hungarian public collection of art. Although its halls have been remodelled several times, the building has always served as a museum. Behind the square is City Park, one of Budapest's largest, with nearly a full square kilometre of green. The bridge leading to the park was also built in 1896 for the Millennial Exhibition. The lake, laid with concrete in 1908, is open for boating in the summer and is host to winter skating. In the distance is a replica of Vajdahunyad Castle in Transylvania, designed by Ignác Alpár and one of the main attractions at the Millennial Exhibition.

Walking down the square toward the monument and passing the great stone tablet dedicated to the memory of the nation's heroes we find ourselves standing face to face with the equestrian statue of Árpád. He is surrounded by the other six tribal leaders of the conquering Magyars. Going left around the base of the column where the warriors stand we read their names: Kond, Ond, Tétény (also known as Töhötöm), Tas, Huba and Előd.

The Magyars, a Finno-Ugric people, reached the Carpathian Basin after a long, venturesome journey. Their original homeland was probably in Western Siberia, an area of high forest extending along the lower reaches of the Ob, from where they moved progressively south. In the course of the first millennium BC, they split from the

30. The tribal leaders of the conquering Magyars

Ob-Ugrian group, and it was at this time that they began to refer to themselves by the name Magyar. For reasons yet obscure, between 500 BC and AD 550 they migrated to the area of modern Bashkiria, a region delineated by the Volga and Kama rivers and the Ural Mountains. The entire region later became known as *Magna Hungaria*. Approximately the same time the Magyars probably divided into seven tribes known as the Nyék, Megyer, Kér, Kürtgyarmat, Tarján, Jenő, and Keszi. In the mid-8th century the Magyars once again moved on, settling in Levedia in the region of the Don. Some of them remained in *Magna Hungaria*, later to be discovered by Friar Julian, the monk who had gone in search of the original homeland in the 13th century.

In Levedia the Magyars fell under the domination of the Khazar Empire. The leader of the Khazars, the *khagan*, entrusted their leadership to a prince known as the *kende*. Real power, however, was concentrated in the hands of the *gyula*, a leader elected by the tribal organization. He was all the more powerful since he was in charge of matters relating to war. Known also in the histories of other peoples, this system became known as the dual principality.

In the mid-9th century the Magyars broke from the Khazar Empire. They extended their area of settlement from the lower Danube to the Southern Carpathians. This was the first independent area of the Hungarian people administered by a strong tribal order. The new country became

31. The Treaty of Pusztaszer *by Gyula Rudnay*

known as Etelköz. Here the Magyars lived in peaceful coexistence with the Khabars, a Turkic tribe which had likewise broken away from Khazar rule. The power of the Hungarian ruler was significantly increased under Levedi and later under Álmos. Tribal merger and unification effected through an alliance was sealed in blood, the "Blood Pact", which has been handed down to us in the form of a historical saga. The Magyars made several raids westward, into the Carpathian Basin and surrounding areas.

Although the Magyars had been preparing for quite some time to occupy the Carpathian Basin, the final move was not the sole result of a voluntary decision. An attack by the Pechenegs provided the impetus for the founders of the country to seek a new

site. The first settlers numbered about half a million. The approximately 200,000 Avars, Bulgar-Alans and Slovenes in the area did not present a serious threat to the occupation; they quickly joined the Magyars, with a significant number of them assimilating to Magyar customs and language.

At that time Kurszán held the office of *kende,* occupying the area of what is today known as Óbuda. The *gyula,* or military leader, was Árpád, who settled the area which is today Pécs. Each of the tribal leaders extended his domain over a given area of the country.

The system of dual principality came to a rather abrupt end. During the course of occupying the Carpathian Basin, the Magyars had come into conflict with states

36

lying west of them. Kurszán set out for the western frontier to negotiate a peace treaty with legates from the Eastern Frankish Empire. But upon their arrival at the ceremonial feast, Kurszán and his men were ambushed and treacherously murdered by the peace envoys. Thus, in 904, the Magyars were left with only Árpád. His rule was further assured by the pledges made in the Blood Pact that the Hungarian ruler was always to be selected from among the offspring of Álmos. Since Árpád was Álmos's son, the Árpád clan was thereby popularly regarded as having a permanent claim to leadership. Hungarian folklore imbues the Árpád family with miraculous powers. In totemistic societies, tribes choose an animal as their ancestor. The Árpád clan considered

the *hawk*—by its Turkic name *turul*—as their ancestral father, and employed the myth in affirming the superhuman origins of the dynasty. Nevertheless, most likely the decisive factor in Árpád's bid for power was that he actually held the greatest military power. His military might is further attested to by the fact that in 904 he was able to claim the Roman amphitheatre in Óbuda, which came to be known as Kurszán's fort, for his estate immediately upon taking power. He also established a power base west of the Danube, and in 907 was victorious in battle against the encroaching forces of the Eastern Franks and Bavarians, securing power for the Magyars over the newly-won lands. He was buried in Óbuda.

The Magyars did not find it easy adapt-

32. The Magyar Conquest *by Mihály Munkácsy*

33. King Stephen the Saint

turned and proceeded to shower them with arrows. The enemy's numbers having been severely decimated, it had virtually no chance for retreat. As knowledge of the fighting tactics of the Magyars spread and the political situation in the West consolidated, the Age of Adventures drew to a close in the latter half of the 10th century. In order to survive, only one option lay open to the Magyars and that was to establish a state conforming to the standards of contemporary Europe, as established by Christianity and feudalism.

In 972 Géza became ruler over the Hungarians. He concluded a peace treaty with the expanding German Empire and agreed to accept Christian missionaries sent into the country. With his marriage to Sarolta, daughter of the *Gyula* of Transylvania, he managed to secure Transylvania as part of Hungary. Defeating rebellious tribal leaders in Transdanubia, he secured major areas through military force. He established the seat of his rule in Esztergom.

Located on the Danube, Esztergom had been an inroad for the flow of western goods and customs. The Hungarian statesman who occupies the first place on the left-hand colonnade in the monument was

ing to a settled agrarian life. They made continuous raids out of the Carpathian Basin, foraging westward and south; the chronicles record 43 such raids of incursion. The Magyars at one time held all of Europe for ransom, from the Iberian Peninsula to Byzantium. In addition to the political unrest and confusion in the area, a further reason for their repeated military success was their unorthodox military tactics. Only the upper ranks wielded sabres, with simple horsemen fighting with bow and arrow, and battle-axes, working in small units which fought very efficiently. First a tremendous shower of arrows rained upon the enemy. The Magyars then staged a retreat, drawing the enemy forward. They then, standing upright in their saddles,

34. The coronation of St Stephen

35. The Holy Crown

born in Esztergom during the first half of the 970s. At birth he received the pagan name Vajk (meaning "lesser chieftain"), but was later baptized with the name István or Stephen. Following the death of Géza, Stephen ascended to power, in accordance with feudal tradition which stipulated that power was to pass to the eldest *son*. However, his ascension was called into question, since according to ancient Hungarian tradition, the oldest *member* of the family was in line for succession. His rule was thus challenged by Koppány, the eldest member of the Árpád clan. Stephen ultimately secured his rights to the crown in armed combat, defeating Koppány, and then, in a show of power, displayed each part of the quartered body in the different sections of the country. In efforts to consolidate power after his victory, Stephen asked to be crowned by the Pope. His request was granted, and on Christmas Day, in the year 1000, he was crowned at Székesfehérvár, which became the royal seat of power. With this historical act Hungary embarked on membership in the community of Christian European states.

Here mention must be made of the crown which for centuries has occupied a vital place in Hungarian history. The Holy Crown, which is today in the National Museum, Budapest, was, to the best of our knowledge, never worn by Saint Stephen. Over the course of time the original crown had fallen into the hands of the Holy Roman Emperor Henry III, who reputedly sent it to Rome, after which time its whereabouts became unknown. That is why either Andrew II and Géza I—both of whom had been at war with the Holy Roman Emperor in the 11th century—had turned to Byzantium for a crown. The lower, circular part of the crown originates from the court of the Byzantine Emperor, Michael Dukas. When the upper part of the crown was attached cannot be asserted with any authority, and is currently the subject of much debate. All that can be claimed with any certainty is that the form of the crown, as we know it today, has occurred in representations from the 15th century onwards. Perhaps more vital to the crown's history is its symbolic value over the centuries as a holy and venerable object, representing Hungarian statehood, independence, and constitutionality. The crown had originally been intended to represent the fact that the constitutionality of the land was determined by the unity of the king and estates, a function which was also expressed during the coronation ceremony. Later, after the elimination of feudalism, it became an expression of territorial unity. The symbolism of the crown is employed in the monument, where it appears in the right hand of Gabriel. After a rather checkered history, the priceless crown is back in Budapest and has become a museum piece of inestimable value.

Once Stephen had been crowned, he received papal mandate to establish the church orders. This could not be accomplished without foreign assistance, since the majority of Hungarians, who were still pagan, were slow to accept the new faith. This resistance to conversion acquired all the more impetus since the spread of Christianity ran concomitant with the transformation of tribal society. Bishoprics were established on royal estates. Stephen's intent to establish the state is also manifest in the fact that Esztergom was accorded archiepiscopal rank in 1001, thereby averting the danger of the newly established Hungarian church falling under the power of the German archbishopric. Albeit with foreign assistance, Stephen was able to achieve the state

36. *King Ladislas the Saint*

independence he had set out for. As the church gained a greater foothold andStephen's power increased, he turned his eforts to putting down rebellions in Transylvania and the Temes region. He did become ruler over the entire country, as indicated by the fact that he established an administrative organization, a system of royal counties based on royal holdings comprising two-thirds of all lands. His laws defended the church, Christians, and the royal estates, at the same time condemning tribal traditions. Among the tribal practices they sought to eliminate was the principle of the *talion,* "eye for eye, tooth for tooth". In his foreign policy Stephen likewise strove to ensure that the Hungarian kingdom would enjoy full legitimacy as a state in Christian Europe. Through war, and the building of dynastic relations, he established the country's stability and gained international recognition. Hungary became an independent state in the shadow of two great powers, the Byzantine and Holy Roman Empires.

When Stephen died in 1038, he could rest assured of having finished what his father, Géza, had begun. He had organized the people into a state, thus ensuring them a permanent place in history. In 1083 Pope Gregory VII canonized Stephen, along with his son Emeric whose death took place under mysterious circumstances, and Bishop Gellért (Gerard), martyred during his missionary activity in Hungary. The anniversary of King Stephen's canonization has been celebrated since the 11th century on August 20th, the date officially set aside in his honour.

The final phase of consolidating the medieval Hungarian state is associated with Kings Ladislas and Coloman the Beauclerc, whose statues stand along that of King Stephen in the Millennial Monument. The struggles for the throne following Stephen's death, attacks from outside, and internal revolt endangered the great king's achievements. Successful wars of defence in this period prevented Hungary from falling un-

38. The reliquary of St Ladislas

37. St Ladislas slaying the Cumanian abductor

der the power of the German Empire, while the quelling of internal revolt ensured that Stephen's accomplishments would not fall by the wayside.

When Ladislas I ascended the throne in 1077 all of Europe was divided by the struggle between the papacy and the empire. Henry IV had made humble submission to Pope Gregory VII in 1077 at Canossa, and the up and down struggle between the two powers went on. Since there was more to fear from the German Empire, Ladislas naturally allied himself with the Pope. But when relations in that sphere also deteriorated, he made political overtures to the Emperor as well. His laws contributed to the dependence of freemen on landlords, and reinforced the holding of private property in the feudal system. Those seeking to escape the expanding power of

39. King Coloman the Beauclerc

predecessor, he consolidated the authority of the Hungarian throne over Slavonia, Croatia, and Dalmatia. Croatia remained a possession of the Hungarian crown until 1918, preserving its internal self-government while formally being tied to the Hungarian ruler. In the struggle between papacy and empire, Coloman was a firm supporter of the Pope, in this case, breaking with the precedent set by his predecessor. Nevertheless, he carried on the work of Ladislas in his relentless defence of private property, and in the juridical administration conceived in the name of that defence. Popular opinion associated enlightened thought with the hunchback king, and out of respect for his laws and education accorded him the additional title of *Könyves* (Beauclerc).

In major respects the Hungary of the 12th century was already feudal, characterized predominantly by agrarian communities. There was a network of some 4,000–5,000 villages, their inhabitants numbering from 80 to 100 each. Lands were held by the king, the Church or private landowners. The latter group increasingly provided tenants with a house, plot, and the necessary tools for production in exchange for a part of their yield and labour.

The overwhelming majority of people

the landlords fled to the borderlands, an opportunity the king seized upon to ensure his claim to power over the entire Carpathian Basin. The death of his sister's husband, the King of Croatia, provided the ideal opportunity to make Croatia part of the Hungarian kingdom. Ladislas drove back the Uz, ethnically related to the Cumans, and the Pechenegs, who had attacked on the eastern flank. Numerous sagas record the deeds of the king as he waged wars to preserve the nation. According to popular belief he appeared after his death in 1095, and many miracles were recorded having taken place at his tomb in Nagyvárad. He was subsequently canonized in 1192.

Succeeding Ladislas, Coloman reigned until 1116. Following in the footsteps of his

40. Coloman the Beauclerc prohibiting the burning of witches

41. Coloman the Beauclerc Issues the Decree Prohibiting the Burning of Witches *by Zsigmond Vajda*

living in the country were Hungarian. The ethnic groups who had been in the country at the time of settlement had assimilated to Hungarian ways. Ishmaelites from the east, Germans settling in the Szepes region and in Transylvania, and settlements of Italians, Walloons, and Flemish scattered across the country added local flavour to ethnic composition, but did not basically modify them. The second half of the 12th century marks the beginning of the Wallachian migration into Transylvania from the south which by the 14th and 15th centuries had taken on massive proportions. The Slovakian peoples formed in the north from a mixture of Slavic ethnic groups, while the Ruthenians began to appear in the north.

During the period of internal dissent and struggle over succession, kings began the practice of making land grants in order to win followers, and slowly but surely the royal counties also fell victim to dispensation. The influence of large secular and church estates and political power was growing at the expense of the power of the king. Andrew II, who had ascended the throne in 1205, continued the practice of securing followers by making land grants. The ever-powerful large landowners, unsatisfied with what they had received from the king, attempted to sway the influence of the royal *servientes*. The *servientes* were an independent group of free small landowners who provided military service to the king, and were in possession of the seized area of royal counties in the vicinity of the large estates. In addition, owners of medium-sized estates had also been threatened by the expansion of the larger estates. At the same time, the king, in order to increase the revenue which had fallen off due to the landgrants, had resorted to the devaluation

42. *King Andrew II*

of the coin. Ever newer currencies were created, each of successively lower value, while the king justified the increase of revenue as necessary for the exchequer.

These new sums of money flowing into the exchequer were not put to good use. Following the example of King Coloman, Andrew II made an abortive attempt to conquer Galicia. His crusades to the Holy Land likewise won little glory for the crown. His wife, the Meranian Gertrude, ran a lavish, wasteful household. Andrew II's rule triggered widespread unrest, and in 1213 Gertrude was assassinated by a high-level conspiracy. The king's inefficacy was further testified to by the fact that he was unable to punish the assassins. Andrew II's political opponents formed an alliance,

43. The Proclamation of the Golden Bull *by Mátyás Jantyik*

forcing him to ratify the Golden Bull of 1222, named for the golden seal which hung from it. The document guaranteed rights to the *servientes* which had formerly only been enjoyed by the owners of great estates and also contained the famous "clause of resistance", whereby if the king failed to keep his word, the nobles were invested with the right to resist and oppose him without charge of disloyalty.

The Golden Bull of 1222—held by King Andrew in the statue sculpted for the Millennial Monument—for all purposes determined the principle of equality between nobles and occupied a central place in the thought of the Hungarian aristocracy for

centuries. Although subsequently repealed, the clause of resistance initiated the long-term practice of throwing open the acts of the king to question. Because of the seminal role it played in the development of national constitutionality, the Golden Bull has frequently been likened to the Magna Charta of 1215, underscoring certain clear parallels in the constitutional development of Hungary and England.

Andrew II was too weak to enforce the decrees of the Golden Bull. An absentee king could not defend the interests of his *servientes vis-à-vis* the large landowners, who, consequently, responded by electing their own magistrates. In 1232, the king

44. King Andrew II setting out for the Crusade

45. The Golden Bull

45

46. *King Béla IV*

would be in his best interests to crown the boy himself. The eight-year-old child became known as the 'junior king'. Fearing that his son would be used as a pawn against him, the king sent him abroad at the time of the crusades. But when it came time for the boy to be married, relations between father and son were marred by the father's intolerable posture to his son's marriage. Andrew had betrothed his son to the daughter of the Greek Nicene emperor, Maria Laskaris. The fourteen-year-old child went on to marry his Maria, only to find himself ordered two years later by his father to drive away his wife in order to secure the advantages of a second marriage. The church defended the indivisibility of the nuptial bond, while Béla, since he loved his wife, took her back to the kingdom. Andrew II at last recognized the marriage in order to avoid armed conflict.

As junior king, Béla ruled in Slavonia and later in Transylvania. He felt his father's policies to be erroneous and believed that the practice of land grants weakened the monarchy rather than secured advantages for it. He made it his goal to regain the royal estates that his father had given away.

legitimized this practice by granting, for the first time, the right to the *servientes* of Zala County to select their own magistrate. This initiated the historical process whereby the system of royally administered counties was gradually replaced with those which came under the jurisdiction of nobles. The fact that nobles were allowed to exercise autonomy within their counties was a central feature of Hungarian administration up to the mid-19th century.

Andrew's son, Béla IV, grew up in the insecure circumstances of the court. He had been only seven years old when his mother, the queen had been assassinated. The noblemen involved in the assassination had sought to replace Andrew II by putting his son on the throne. The king decided it

47. *King Béla IV rebuilds the country after the Mongol Invasion*

Overruling the earlier grants, he confiscated, among others the possessions which had been seized by his mother's assassins, thus attempting to put the throne on a sounder footing. During his father's lifetime, he was only partially able to realize his plans. When Andrew II suddenly died in September of 1235, Béla hastened to Székesfehérvár to have himself crowned a second time as the sole monarch of the land.

He set about restoring law and order to the land with an authoritative hand. He demanded absolute submission, a fact expressed even in the outward details of ceremony. He forbade the peers of the land, barring the prelates, to sit in his presence at the royal council, and had the superfluous seats burnt. He straightened out matters involving those living on royal estates, and substantially increased royal holdings, and even confiscated land from the Church.

Béla's policies created considerable tension and actually had a detrimental impact on the country at a time when unity was needed, as the expansion of the Mongol empire was becoming an increasing threat to Hungary. The Khan demanded Béla's surrender. However, Béla not only refused but he also provided safe haven to the Cumans who had fled with their ruler after having been routed by the Mongols. That the Cumans were a nomadic and the Hungarians an agrarian people soon led to clashes: the prince of the Cumans, Kötöny, was assassinated, and his people fled the country, pillaging as they left. Thus instead of strengthening the country, Béla had unintentionally weakened it.

The Mongol attack was overwhelming. The king's army was annihilated at the village of Mohi along the Sajó River on April 11, 1241. The Mongols pressed forward

48. *The Mongol Invasion as represented in the* Illuminated Chronicle

along the Danube. Having gone into exile, the king's request for assistance went unheeded, the Austrian prince even went so far as to exact a ransom from him. In the winter of 1241–42, the Mongols crossed the Danube. Only a few fortified stone castles were able to muster resistance. Béla IV sought refuge in Dalmatia at Trau (today Trogir) Castle. His pursuers had swept as far as the seacoast, when in the spring of 1242 they unexpectedly turned back and after the death of the chief Khan, abandoned the conquered country, leaving in their wake massive destruction. Many observers were convinced that Hungary as a country had ceased to exist.

Béla set about the enormous task of rebuilding the country. He called back the Cumans and resettled them. Abandoning his earlier policy, he gave the landlords and the Church large land-grants to assist them in building castles capable of providing defence in the event of a renewed Mongol attack. He extended aid to the cities, which not only took the form of financial but of military assistance as well, providing them with fortified citadels. The defence of the nation's borders was entrusted to crusaders who were rewarded in turn with large estates. He abandoned the centuries-old attempt to secure Galicia and formed an alliance with the prince.

The power of individual lords of great estates thus grew to enormous proportions, renewing the danger of disunity. In an attempt to prevent this, he granted nobility to the *servientes* in 1267 and recognized the administrative authority of nobles in their respective counties. The nobility won the right to send delegates from each county seat to the judicial sessions of the royal assizes. In 1269, Béla made an alliance with the Angevin House of Naples, descended from the French Angevin line, securing dynastic ties by marrying his granddaughter to a Neapolitan Angevin prince, and his grandson to Isabella of Naples. His attempts to rebuild the country, however, were diverted by his conflict with his son. Stephen was also bent on ruling and in the face of military opposition, his father was forced to concede power. Béla had good reason to believe that strife in the family would only favour the increasing power of the oligarchs, and the threat of disunity would jeopardize all the accomplishments of the years of reconstruction. He spent his latter years on Margaret Island, once known as Rabbit's Island, at the side of his daughter, Margaret, where he died on May 3, 1270. The inscription on the tomb of the king, who is regarded as the second founder of the Hungarian state, reads: "During his reign, cunning ceased, peace prospered, and honour prevailed."

Béla IV's successors were not able to forestall the power of the oligarchs. These lords had carved out their own separate territories, minted their own coins, and generally acted in the manner of autono-

49. King Charles Robert

mous rulers. When the last ruler of the Árpád House, Andrew III, died in 1301, the issue of succession was raised. Attempts on the throne came from all sides. One of those laying claim to the throne, Charles Robert, was descended from the Angevin line. Resting his claim on a 1269 pact with Béla IV, he was recognized, after a long struggle, as the sole lawful king of Hungary in 1308.

Both Charles Robert and his successor, Louis the Great, are representative of the 14th-century domination of Angevin rule in Hungary, and are accordingly shown in the Millennial Monument as the knight kings of the *fleur-de-lis* banner.

During the period roughly extending through the 1320s, Charles Robert waged a successful battle against the political and

48

economic power of the oligarchs. He moved the seat of political power to Visegrád, renowned for its beauty and defensibility in the centre of the country, thus giving clear indication that centralized rule had returned to the hands of the king. The king surrounded himself with aristocrats who could be counted on to put down the power of the oligarchs; in return, they received title, rank and estates. They had further reason to ally with the king since their position was not yet stable enough to rise up against him. Even if they were state dignitaries, in the event of war they were required to muster a certain number of soldiers under their banners. These military units became known as *banderia,* and they served as the country's base of defence. Although the king devoted a portion of his power to reclaiming his estates, he was clearly aware that in this domain he had lost decisive authority. At most he could be first among equals. Therefore he had to seek some other way to replenish the royal coffers.

Most of the revenue channelled into the exchequer issued from the royal intake of precious metals. This meant, for example, that the king exercised exclusive prerogative over one-tenth of extracted gold and

51. The golden florin of Charles Robert

one-eight of silver. Charles Robert allowed landlords who had quarries on their estates to retain one-third of the profits. This stimulated exploration of new mines, which in turn saw an upswing in the mining of precious metals. At this time Hungary produced 40 per cent of the world's gold and 30 per cent of its silver. Duties on trade also increased royal revenue.

With the stabilizing of the economic situation, Charles Robert was able to implement one of his major reforms, the introduction of new money. Prior to the reform, some 35 domestic and foreign types of money had been in regular circulation. The situation during conversion and redemption was one of general confusion, since rates were not regulated, and the ratio between unminted silver to standard weight had not yet been established. The king issued a new currency—the golden florin *(forint)*, after the Florentine model. Not long after the change in currency, a silver *garas* was also issued, which was patterned after the Czech coinage.

The introduction of a stable system of currency brought an end to the royal practice of devaluing currency. In its place, the ruler introduced a tax on units of land held

50. King Ladislas IV defeating the Czech king, Ottokar, with Rudolf Habsburg. 1278

in villeinage. Towns were also brought under taxation, but in exchange for the added
revenue, he in turn helped to foster their
development. Charters were granted one
after another. At that time towns were
small by modern standards—Buda was the
largest with some 8,000 inhabitants, becoming the royal seat of power by virtue of its
size and importance. Medium-sized towns
had populations of between three and four
thousand people, while smaller ones contained a population of one to two thousand.
A significant number of town-dwellers had
already turned to crafts or trade for their
livelihoods. The king bore in mind their
interests when he initiated a sweeping
foreign policy to bolster trade. By 1335, he
had organized a meeting in Visegrád for the
Czech and Polish kings to promote economic exchange between the three countries, thus avoiding the observance of the
Viennese staple right which demanded mer-
chants passing through the country to un-
load their wares in a specified place. Although this not very covert anti-Austrian
action was not entirely effective, it went far
to promote the development of trade and
towns.

The substantial economic reforms in-
stituted by Charles Robert, following the
subdual of the oligarchs, restored Hungary
to its position as a flourishing kingdom. The
ruler waged relatively few wars, leading
troops primarily into Wallachia and the
Banat of Szörény, the latter of which he
secured. Political consolidation and the climate of stable economic relations led to
balanced population growth, with the
number of inhabitants reaching between
two and two and a half million. The king
also promoted dynastic expansion. His third
wife, Elizabeth Lokietek, was the daughter

52. *King Louis the Great*

of the Polish king, and the marriage fos-
tered recognition of his oldest son, Louis, as
successor to the Polish throne. He married
his younger child, Andrew, to Johanna, heir
to the Neapolitan throne, in hopes of laying
claim to that throne as well.

Charles Robert embodied the ideal of the
knight king. His knightly order was
modelled on the French, and became the
second of its kind in Europe. Life at court
was marked by festive ceremonies and
jousting matches. Not content to be an on-
looker, Charles was a frequent combatant
of tournaments. He always made a point of
generously compensating his defeated opponents. On one occasion, one opponent,
who had lost three teeth in combat, was
awarded three villages in compensation. He

was also a generous patron of the arts. It happened that the goldsmith who made the royal seal was awarded an entire village over the asking price as a reward for his outstanding work. His behaviour served as a chivalric ideal, thus winning acceptance for chivalry among the nobles of the land.

During the course of his reign extending some 40 years (1342–1384), Louis the Great, who had inherited the ideals held up by his father, provided ample proof that he, too, was a chivalric king. Immediately following his coronation, he made a pilgrimage to Várad to the tomb of Saint Ladislas. Ladislas was his inspiration—he had provided him with the ideal of *noblesse oblige,* and Ladislas's exemplary conduct in the struggle against the Cumans had been a source of strength and inspiration for the knights. Ladislas came to be depicted on church frescoes, on the obverse of gold florins, and his likeness was also cast in bronze.

Also in the spirit of knighthood, Louis was bent on revenging the murder of his brother, Andrew, heir apparent to the Neapolitan throne. He had led several military campaigns against Naples and his sister-in-law, Johanna, who had been a party to the assassination of the prince. His military ventures make some of the best stories of the chivalric age recorded in the chronicles, but in spite of the ardent description of these

54. The miracles of St Ladislas, from the Legends of the Hungarian Angevin Kings

53. Louis the Great occupies Naples

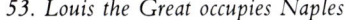

campaigns, the actual military expeditions were largely unsuccessful. Louis captured Naples twice, but in the interests of avoiding encroachment on papal and Venetian rights, he refrained from establishing power. Nevertheless, these military actions cost him a lot of money. As opposed to his father's rule, Louis's term in power was marked by an aggressive military policy. His generals had been sent to war thirteen times, and he had personally led the troops into battle another sixteen times. In his Balkan campaign, he extended provisional rule over Dalmatia, Serbia, Bosnia, and Bulgaria. It was here that clashes are recorded with the Turks, with the Angevin king proving the victor. He secured the Polish crown by right of succession, thus linking

51

55. Louis the Great with the foundation deed of Kassa Cathedral

the two countries through the person of a single monarch. It was under his rule that the Hungarian frontier was extended the farthest, at that time comprising the seacoasts of the Adriatic, Baltic, and the Black Seas.

His laws proved more enduring than his military exploits. The 1351 legal code contained three laws which remained on the statutes until 1848. Protection was extended to the small and medium-sized holdings against the expansion of the larger estates. In an entailment provision, he decreed the inviolability of noble landholdings. The provision specified that after the male line on the estate had died out, the estate was to be transferred to the collateral line, and after the decease of the entire family, the estate was to be returned to the royal domain. A single mandatory tax was ordered for the entire land, whereby one-ninth of the serf's yields were to be given over to the landlord. The new provision laid down the principle of equality for all noblemen of the land.

The ideal of the chivalric king was also

56. János Hunyadi

reflected in Louis's patronage of sciences and the arts. In 1367 he founded the University of Pécs, which flourished for a brief period. His court bustled with the coming and going of painters, master builders, and physicians. He set about building a large palace in Buda; during excavation a considerable number of findings were made from the Angevin period. A large library was discovered; some of the most handsome works in the collection included the *Legends of the Hungarian Angevin Kings* and the *Illuminated Chronicle,* two masterpieces of European bookmaking. After having acquired the posthumous title 'Great' in the 15th and 16th centuries, he has been referred to ever since as Louis the Great.

After his death his younger daughter Ma-

ria ascended the throne. The empowered barons took the opportunity to form leagues bent on weakening the power of the throne to further their own influence. Neither Maria's husband, Sigismund, nor five subsequent rulers could amass enough power to break the hold of the barons. All this time a much more threatening power had been assembling on the southern border of the country. In 1439 the Turks occupied the whole of Serbia, and all that separated them from Hungary was the Danube.

King Wladislas I, descended from the House of Jagiello, had that year named János Hunyadi to the unenviable post of governor of the region threatened by the Turks, the Banat of Szörény. The decisive role that Hunyadi would play in history was later to ensure him a place in the Millennial Monument. After having come into conflict with the pro-Turkish policy of the *boyars,* Hunyadi's father had fled to Hungary from Wallachia. In 1409, he received Hunyad Castle from Sigismund in repayment for his services, and from that time on the family took the name Hunyadi. Already as a young man Hunyadi had taken part in the anti-Turkish wars. He made up the king's retinue on official visits to Italy and Bohemia. In Italy, he became schooled in the art of mercenary fighting, while becoming ac-

57. The Battle of Nándorfehérvár

58. The Battle of Nándorfehérvár *by Mátyás Jantyik*

quainted with the military fighting tactics of the Hussites from the Czechs. He was reputed to be an invincible warrior, a title he earned on the southern frontier. In addition to the Banat of Szörény, he was also awarded the Voivodeship of Transylvania, the Banat of Temes, and became captain of Belgrade. His newly acquired posts also enabled him to increase his landholdings, as he was lord over some 30 castles, 60 boroughs, 1,000 villages, and some two million hectares. In the anti-Turkish wars, he was able to put his huge fortune to good use. In 1442, at Gyulafehérvár, he inflicted a crushing defeat on the encroaching Turkish forces. His victory was all the more significant since it went far to break the illusion of the invincible Turkish army.

The following year he embarked on another campaign, this time to expel the Turks from Europe. Although he did not achieve his goals, he was able to extract unusually favourable peace terms from the Sultan. Upon the solicitation of the papacy and Venice, Wladislas broke the treaty and renewed the offensive against the Turks; this campaign was halted by the Battle of Varna in 1444. Wladislas died in battle and the Christian forces were annihilated. Internal dissension broke out within the country, the Turks, assessing the situation, made new preparations for conquest.

Hunyadi's followers sought to have him elected regent during the period of the new king's absence from the court, as Ladislas V was still a minor. Hunyadi occupied this position until 1453. Allied with the ruler of the Albanians, Skander Bey, Hunyadi rallied forces against the Turks, but in spite of a heroic attempt at Rigómező treachery and the sheer numbers of his opponent forced him to retreat. The extremely talented and ambitious Mehmed II had assumed power in the Turkish camp. In order for the Sultan to secure the Balkan and break through the frontier defence of Hungary, he needed to take Belgrade.

In 1456 the scene was set for a major battle. With some 150 thousand troops, the Turks besieged Belgrade (Nándorfehérvár), the gate to Hungary and, thus, to all of Christian Europe. Troops garrisoned at Belgrade totalled to only 5,000 men. Cognizant of the enormity of the threat, the Pope decreed a crusade. The Franciscan fathers assisted in recruiting crusaders, who were put under the command of John Capistrano. Hunyadi assembled a relief force and, by mid-July, had arrived in Belgrade with 10,000 men. In a week's time, on July 21, the Turks launched a massive attack. The battle lasted throughout the night. Hunyadi put up an exceptionally brave struggle, assuming the roles of leader and fighter. Just as the horse-tailed banner of the Turks was being raised to the castle wall, one of the soldiers, Titus Dugovics, in an act of heroism, lunged at the Turkish soldier, dragging them both to their death.

The following day the Hungarians broke out of the castle, fighting attacks and counter-attacks; by nightfall, Hunyadi had given the command to withdraw, thinking it risky to pass the night in such close proximity to the besieging army. Hunyadi had planned to attack on the following morning, but the Turks had already disappeared. Observing Hunyadi's dauntlessness and weighing the losses his army had suffered, the Sultan had ordered his troops to retreat. Not long after the victory was hailed across Europe, Hunyadi fell victim to the plague epidemic which had swept through the camp. At the news of the victory, the Pope issued a proclamation for the noon bell to be rung throughout Christendom to proclaim Hunyadi's triumph, a custom which is still observed. Hunyadi's victory at Belgrade made it possible to stall renewed Turkish conquests of Hungary for some 70 years.

As a result of the internal strife following upon his death, Hunyadi's older son was executed, while the younger, Matthias, was banished to Prague. In November of 1457 Ladislas V died of the plague. With the question of succession open to dispute, the

59. The coat of arms of János Hunyadi

60. King Matthias Corvinus (Hunyadi)

Habsburgs and Jagiellos made successive bids to place an heir on the throne. The popular choice of the estates fell to 15-year-old Matthias Hunyadi. Under the leadership of Mihály Szilágyi, Matthias's uncle, Hunyadi's supporters marched to the electoral Diet with 15,000 soldiers. The scene staged to threaten the electorate achieved the desired end, and Matthias was proclaimed king.

Matthias's reign marks the last flourishing period of Hungarian statehood for some centuries to come. The country's population rose to between 3.5 and 4 million, while, compared to those of previous reigns, royal revenues quadrupled, comprising an annual total of some 800,000 forints. These population figures and re-

venues of the exchequer were approximately on a par with those of contemporary England. Substantial revenues made it possible to call up a mercenary army loyal only to the king, otherwise known as the 'Black Army' for the black uniforms they wore. The king established an administration answerable solely to him. He levied a heavy tax burden on the peasantry, nevertheless in Hungarian folktales and popular memory, Matthias is renowned as a just king for his staunch defence of the serfs against the abuses of local landlords. Both the Black Army and the king's administration insured those of non-noble origin with the chance to rise in society.

Matthias's consolidation of the country's strength took quite some time. He was victorious in protracted struggles with the baronial leagues, internal rebels, and those who attempted to use him as a pawn. Wars against the Turks were primarily used to fortify already won positions. The focal point of his foreign policy was turned westward in efforts to create a strong Central European empire. He won the claim to the Czech throne and entered into agreement with Frederic of the Habsburg dynasty. Frederic, who had made a bid for the Hungarian throne, had the Holy Crown restored

62. King Matthias in the company of his scholars

62. King Matthias Dispensing Justice *by Zsigmond Vajda*

to Matthias, thus renouncing his claim to rule. In exchange for the crown, he received 60,000 forints and a document wherein Matthias agreed that, in the event of his death with no male successor, the Habsburgs would succeed to the Hungarian throne. Frederic was 48 years old and Matthias 20, and thus a Habsburg claim to the throne seemed a far-off, unlikely possibility. Relations between Frederic and Matthias deteriorated to such an extent that they went to war, and in 1485 Matthias occupied Vienna, took the title of Prince of Austria, and spent the last five years of his life governing his extensive empire from Frederic's former seat.

Matthias was not so fortunate, however, in his domestic life. In his youth, he was wedded to the daughter of one of the leaders of the baronial leagues. She died three months after the marriage. His second wife, the daughter of the Czech king, also died at a young age. Consistent with his foreign policy, at the end of 1476, he wedded Beatrix, the 21-year old daughter of Ferdinand of Aragon, king of Naples. She was not able to provide him with children.

Beatrix's arrival at court marked the beginning of the influence of the Italian Renaissance on Hungarian art, life and manners, a style which proved to be close to Matthias's own cast of mind. The king's taste for the Renaissance was already apparent at the time of the marriage: Matthias attended to all the details of the marriage which became widely talked about across

Europe; he personally saw to every detail from the garments of the pages to the staging of the procession itself. Second only to the pope's, his library, which contained some 2,500 richly illuminated volumes, was renowned the world over. He spent a reputed 33,000 gold florins a year bringing in new acquisitions. The constellations painted on the ceiling of the library stood in the very conjunction they had at the time he was proclaimed king of Bohemia. One can still recognize elements of Renaissance at his castle in Visegrád, despite its state of ruin.

In the last years of his life he devoted enormous energy to having his weak, illegitimate son, János Corvin, recognized as successor. He endowed the boy with an enormous fortune and had the landlords

64. István Bocskai

63. Stove tile with the likeness of King Matthias

swear allegiance to him. In early April, 1490, the 47-year-old king suffered a stroke. On the morning of April 6, after two days of suffering, he died. No sooner had he closed his eyes, than the landlords retracted their oaths. Thus the process of liquidating Matthias's inheritance, ushered in the decline of the Hungarian state.

In 1526, the Hungarian army suffered a crushing defeat by the Turks at Mohács. Buda fell in 1541, signalling the end of Hungary's existence as an independent state. The country was divided into three sections: the Turks occupied the central and southern regions of the country; in the east, the independent principality of Transylvania came into existence; and the northern and western regions together with Croatia and Slavonia came under the rule of the Habsburgs, who had secured their claim to the throne. The latter area was known as the Kingdom of Hungary.

The country found itself caught between the two great powers, the Habsburgs and the Turks. The population diminished. Hungary became a military arena where soldiers from West and East locked forces in combat. While the Turks presented the threat and the challenge of a new culture, the Habsburgs sought to defend the interests of their empire through promotion of the Counter-Reformation. Up to this time, the majority of Hungarians converted to Protestantism. The forced re-conversion to Catholicism and resistance to it greatly aggravated the existing Hungarian–Habsburg conflict.

The first hero of national independence, István Bocskai, also occupies an important place in the Millennial Monument. His fortunes embodied all of the tensions of late 16th-century Hungary. Bocskai was a high-born aristocrat who began his political career in Transylvania. His main objective in the 1590s was the expulsion of the Turks. Realizing that the Ottoman Empire was losing its foothold, in his office as senior administrator of Transylvania, he made an alliance with the Austrian emperor to expel the Turks. The Habsburg emperor, how-

66. István Bocskai's crown

ever, withheld the promised assistance, abandoning Transylvania to the onslaught of the Turks. The small country flourishing at that time subsequently became a devastated battlefield. By this time Bocskai was no longer in Transylvania. He had been relieved of his post, and when he protested against the actions of the imperial general who had dealt unmercifully with the civilians, he was imprisoned. Upon his return, he witnessed the Habsburgs' aggressive drive to spread the Catholic faith. A great number of serfs had fled from the war and the drive toward Catholic conversion, while the Emperor had discharged the peasants who had enlisted with the Imperial Army. These peasants banded together to become known as the *Hajdú,* a term associated in the Hungarian language with the cattle drivers on the Great Plains.

In the fall of 1604, Count Belgiojoso, imperial captain-general of Kassa, decided to secure the Bocskai fortune, one of the largest landholdings in eastern Hungary, for the royal family. Accusing Bocskai of high treason, he set forth with an army of 10,000 men to enforce his claim. By this time the

65. Bocskai's Hajdú *soldiers fighting the emperor's mercenaries*

restless *Hajdú*, disenfranchised serfs, had fled to the side of Bocskai, lord of Bihar County. Soon the aristocracy and nobility also joined in the by now openly anti-Habsburg fight for freedom to repay the lack of military support against the Turks and unrestituted feudal and religious grievances. In April of 1605, at the Diet of Szerencs, Bocskai was elected ruling prince of Hungary. The power relations between the Turkish and Habsburg Empires did not afford much opportunity for national independence. Nevertheless, Bocskai and his army of 30,000 won important victories.

The Treaty of Vienna in 1606 provided autonomy for Habsburg-ruled Hungary, specifying that only Hungarian high officials and not the king's foreign advisors were entitled to govern the country—irrespective of religious affiliation—and guaranteeing the right to name Hungarian captains to the frontier castles engaged in the struggle against the Turks. The peace with the emperor also provided that solely Hungarian laws would be binding in Hungary. Feudal grievances were redressed, cases of high treason dismissed, and freedom of religion secured for the nobility, towns, and frontier castles. At the same time Bocskai liberated the main core of his troops—the loyalist *Hajdú*—from serfdom, invested them with communal rights, and settled them in areas which later came to be known as *Hajdú* towns.

In elevating the *Hajdú*, who served faithfully in defence of national rights, Bocskai had created a core of alliance which could be called on in the future if needed. As a special measure to ensure adherence to the provisions of the Peace Treaty of Vienna applying specifically to Hungary, Bocskai secured recognition of the independence of

67. *Gábor Bethlen*

the principality of Transylvania, insisting that "Transylvania had been the strongest shield raised for the survival of the nation." In a further effort to promote development in both Transylvania and Hungary, he negotiated peace between the Habsburgs and the Turks, bringing about an end to nearly fifteen years of war. Several days after concluding peace with the Turks, he died in December of 1606 in Kassa.

The next figure in the monument is that of Gábor Bethlen, who ruled as prince of Transylvania from 1613. In the 1540s, in Transylvania, the young landed proprietor had fallen under the patronage of Bocskai, who schooled him in diplomacy, war, and policy. As prince of Transylvania, Bethlen set out to establish an independent Hungarian kingdom, modelling his ideal on the strong state set up by Matthias Hunyadi. Well aware that it was not possible to wage successful war with two great powers simultaneously, he maintained good relations with the Turks, convinced that once Hungary had been unified by a greatly fortified Transylvania it would later be able to expel them. Before his impressive plans could be achieved, however, it would be necessary to reorganize the principality. He recovered the crown estates which had been given away in mortgage, and exercised the rights of the exchequer in the areas of mining and tariff imposition. Assistance to trade and industry proved a success. The crown's revenue grew by an annual half million forints, allowing for the establishment of a strong army. Recognizing the need for an enlightened scholarly community in achieving his objectives, Bethlen founded the Academy of Gyulafehérvár, which became a centre of learning on par with the greatest in Europe. Culture, imbued with the spirit of Protestantism—at that time equivalent to national culture—flourished.

The anti-Habsburg insurrection of the Czech feudal estates provided Bethlen with the ideal opportunity for realizing his plans for an independent Hungarian state. Entering into alliance with the Czechs, he turned their loss of the war to his advantage. He

69. The seal of Gábor Bethlen

increased Transylvanian territory by seven counties, while guaranteeing freedom of religion for adherents of Protestantism in the Kingdom of Hungary. He embarked upon European politics by forming alliances with the anti-Habsburg forces in the Thirty Years' War. By launching new campaigns, he secured existing victories and achievements. During the 15 years of his rule, Transylvania ascended to the height of its power and Hungarian culture found a haven for further development. Although unification of Hungary had not been achieved, the desire had been reinforced to maintain state unity and to prevent foreign administration.

The 1670s saw a renewal in the anti-Habsburg movement. The movement had been preceded by an organized baronial conspiracy under the leadership of Palatine Ferenc Wesselényi, against the emperor who had been negotiating with the Turks to the detriment of Hungary. The conspirators were arrested and the leaders executed, with only Ferenc Rákóczi I, Prince of Transylvania, having been spared in return for material compensation.

Following the above events, Emperor Leopold I, claiming that the conspirators

68. Gábor Bethlen forming an alliance with the Czech estates

70. Imre Thököly

the leader of the *Kuruts*. His father had been a member of the Wesselényi conspiracy, and he himself had been forced to flee to Transylvania. From there he returned to northern Hungary and quickly proceeded to occupy the upper part of the country.

The emperor was forced to make concessions and summoned the Diet in Sopron in 1681, at which the feudal constitution was partially restored. However, Protestant religious observance was permitted only in two places in each county. Thököly was still not satisfied and, backed by his men, decided to keep on fighting. In 1682, he married Ilona Zrínyi, the widow of Ferenc Rákóczi I, thereby broadening the financial base of the fight for freedom. By now the fight for freedom had reached its most critical point, with the Turks offering Thököly the crown which he duly refused, adopting the title of Prince of Upper Hungary instead. The new state extended from Transylvania to the Vág River, but was short-lived, lasting for only three years.

Inspired by Thököly's success, in 1683 the Turks embarked on a campaign against Vienna. The besieged city was freed by the Polish King John Sobieski and German troops under the command of Charles of Lorraine. The Habsburgs went into attack. In the face of advancing imperial troops, counties, cities, and lords one after another

had forfeited the feudal constitution, introduced a system of absolute rule in Hungary, headed by a German governor-general. Hungarian soldiers serving at border garrisons—now considered unreliable —were dismissed, while harassment of Protestants was renewed, and those pastors who refused to deny their faith were condemned to the galleys. People were forced to go into hiding in ever-increasing numbers for various reasons, and eventually united to form a kind of chivalrous order, reminiscent of the peasant crusader-insurgents of 1514; they came to be referred to as *Kuruts*. To incite the drive for freedom all that was required was a worthy leader.

In 1678, Imre Thököly—descended from a Protestant landowning family—became

71. *The Battle of Szikszó*

went over to the imperial side to swear allegiance, deserting Thököly and the cause. At the news that the Turks had been driven from Érsekújvár, the *Kuruts* went over *en masse* to the side of the emperor, convinced that at the very least the country had been liberated from one noxious influence. Only Ilona Zrínyi remained loyal defending the Castle of Munkács for three years.

In 1686, after some 145 years of Turkish occupation, the last Turks were finally driven from Buda. While Thököly had enjoyed a brief period of success—he reigned as Prince of Transylvania for two months having been helped to the throne by the Turks in 1690—the 1699 Treaty of Karlowicz for all purposes ended the chapter of Turkish power in Hungary. Thököly was forced into exile. Prolonged illness in his last years prevented him from joining the fight for freedom waged by his stepson, Ferenc Rákóczi II. He died in Nicomedia in 1705. His ashes were brought back to Hungary and interred at the Lutheran church of Késmárk in 1906.

With the liberation of Hungary from Turkish rule, the Habsburgs now turned their attention to setting up an oppressive system of rule. The country was ruled like any other conquered territory, falling under the administration of Viennese officials. Nobles were required to produce deeds of ownership, which were non-existent, and were also required to pay huge amounts in compensation for exemption from military service. Vast tracts of land were bestowed on foreign loyalists to the court. The country was subjected to a military reign of terror with nobles and civilians alike executed under suspicion of conspiracy. Enormous taxes were also levied upon the peasantry, who were also burdened with the

72. *The Turkish army in a Turkish painting*

feeding and transport of the occupying army. In no time Leopold I had succeeded in alienating all segments of society.

The outbreak of the Spanish War of Succession in 1701 provided the occasion for national insurrection. The French–Habsburg rivalry tied down a significant portion of the empire's forces in the west. With the emergence of Ferenc Rákóczi II, the new leader of the fight for freedom, the scene was set for war. His father had been a party to the Wesselényi conspiracy (his maternal grandfather had been executed as part of that same conspiracy), while at his mother's side, he had lived through the siege of Munkács. With the fall of the castle he had been taken from his mother and put into a Jesuit

73. Ferenc Rákóczi II

dered by the Danube and Tisza Rivers, and had made incursions into separately administered, Viennese-controlled Transylvania. To ensure a closer unity between nobility and peasantry, he excused those serfs who were in the army from service on estates, while requiring the rest who had remained on estates to continue in feudal service. He was quick to grasp the importance of religious tolerance among his men and, although he had been raised a Catholic, he refused to tolerate discrimination of other religious groups. Lutheran residents of German-settled Hungarian towns also came to be numbered among the *Kuruts*. Rákóczi made strides in promoting culture: schools were reopened at the time of the fight for freedom and the first Hungarian newspaper, printed in Latin, went into circulation. In order to put the fight for freedom on a sound financial basis, Rákóczi had copper money minted and organized weapons production.

At the Diet of Szécsény in 1705, Hungary changed its government to a feudal confederacy similar to that in Poland. Rákóczi was elected ruling prince and commander-in-chief. The advisory body was known as the senate, but Rákóczi had full authority

monastery to be raised in the spirit of loyalty to the emperor. He was raised to become a courtier, but having been influenced by his friend Miklós Bercsényi and having witnessed the deplorable condition of the country, he assumed the leadership of the insurrection. In May of 1703, at the castle of Brezno in Poland, he issued his famous proclamation calling every true patriot, "highborn or low", to war against imperial despotism. The banner of the fight for freedom was raised with the slogan, *"Cum Deo, patria et libertate"*.

Rákóczi crossed back into the country in June of 1703 with an army made up of soldiers who, like Thököly's men, proudly bore the name *Kuruts*. By 1703, they had liberated Upper Hungary and the area bor-

74. Tamás Esze welcoming Ferenc Rákóczi II on his return from Poland

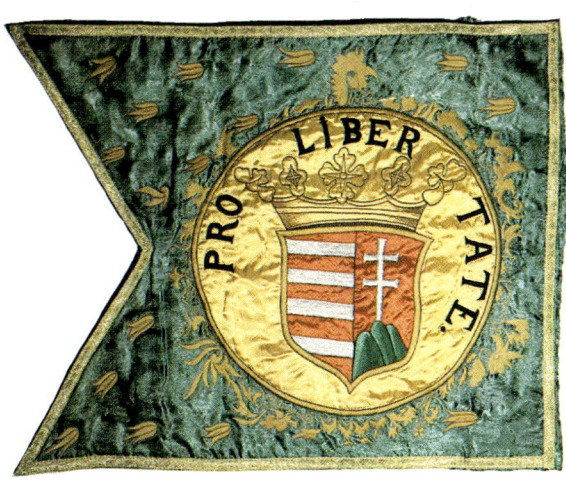

75. *The flag of Ferenc Rákóczi II*

over foreign policy, defence and finance. Terms of agreement with the Habsburgs included the free right of the Hungarian feudal estates to elect their own king and —following the precedent set by Bocskai— the recognition of the autonomy of the principality of Transylvania. Bolstered with the success of military victory, Rákóczi carried these measures a step further at the 1707 Diet of Ónod: upon his recommendation, the estates overthrew the Habsburgs. In addition, for the first time in Hungarian history, the concept of equal taxation was formulated.

Meanwhile the international situation proved rather inhospitable to Hungary's struggle for independence. The French could not be counted on for help; nor had the alliance with Peter the Great brought the expected results. In 1709, the *Kuruts* army had suffered a defeat at Trencsén which sealed their fate. While Rákóczi was seeking help from Peter the Great, one of the captain-generals entered into agreement with the imperial loyalists and signed a peace treaty in 1711 and laid down arms at Majtény. In the Treaty of Szatmár, the em-

peror pledged to honour Hungarian laws and ensure religious freedom for Protestants. Those noblemen swearing allegiance to the emperor would regain or retain already existing estates. The document granted amnesty to Rákóczi as well. Refusing to barter with the enemy, Rákóczi renounced his enormous estates and went into exile. He lived for a time in France and then went on to Turkey. In his memoirs and moral and philosophical tracts, he extolled the virtue of steadfast, compatriot loyalty. He died in Turkey in 1735.

The last statue in the monument is that of Lajos Kossuth. Beneath his statue is inscribed the date 1848–1849, the years of the Hungarian Revolution and War of Independence. This event in the nation's history has been a powerful symbol of national self-determination and civil rights up to the present, and is inevitably associated with the name of Kossuth, the leading statesman in the movement to defeat the Habsburgs.

From the 1830s onwards, bourgeois development had become a major issue in domestic policy. Inspired by liberal principles, reformers waged a campaign for modernization and the guarantee of civil rights. They set out to rescind feudal privileges which presented the main obstacles to national development. They demanded fairer system of taxation, liberation of the serfs, parliamentary representation, governmental responsibility, and freedom of the press. During the reform period in the 1840s, the leadership of the reform camp shifted from the hands of István Széchenyi to Kossuth, a member of the lesser nobility. He proclaimed his views in the *Pesti Hírlap,* a Hungarian daily, which exerted an impact on the nation unlike any other in the history of the Hungarian press. A growing number

65

76. *Lajos Kossuth*

of adherents rallied to the slogan, "Action, rather than re-action."

The Habsburg court regarded the ambitious statesman with suspicion. The omnipotent chancellor Metternich well understood that no ruler exercising absolutist rights could tolerate popular representation and an elected government. He also realized that constitutional restraints would lead to a decreasing in power, thereby threatening the unity of the empire. Consequently, the court could hardly be expected to grant concessions to the movement. Although the reformists had subjected every concern of bourgeois development to scrutiny and prepared proposals for reform, it was virtually impossible to implement the plans.

The Habsburg Empire was shaken by the wave of revolutions which swept through Europe in 1848. March saw the outbreak of the revolution in Vienna and Pest. What was needed were able political figures, such as Kossuth, who could exercise effective leadership. In April 1848, the king was forced to sanction the laws which reformists had fought for in previous years. Now, only the fact of common rule tied the nations together. Kossuth played a decisive role in framing the hard-won laws of April, 1848. As financial minister, he occupied the most difficult, demanding, and important post in the newly formed government. It soon turned out, however, that the achievements of March and April were not to be peacefully realized. At the incitement of the Viennese court, the Ban of Croatia launched and attack on Hungary in September 1848. Executive powers were assumed by the National Defence Council, with Kossuth taking the lead. The Ban was put to flight, but the retreat was quickly followed by an attack waged by the well-trained imperial army. After an initial retreat of the Hungarian army, they later, in the spring of 1849, achieved one success after another. On April 14, 1849, upon the initiative of Kossuth, the National Assembly proclaimed the abolishment of the Habsburg rule. Kossuth became governor. The threatened young ruler, Francis Joseph, suc-

77. *Lajos Kossuth summoning the peasants of the Great Plain to arms*

78. The Diet of 1848 *by Zsigmond Vajda*

ceeded in convincing the Tsar to honour a previous promise. 200,000 Russian soldiers were sent to Hungary to put down the War of Independence. Hungary had only capitulated in its struggle for independence and freedom after falling to the mercy of the two powers. The hopelessly imbalanced contest reached an end in August 1849: the main forces of the Hungarian army surrendered at Világos.

Kossuth continued to rally opposition in emigration, while the absolutist regime used every expedient measure to eradicate the memory of 1848–49. Terror, hanging, massacre and oppression were rampant. Changes in the international scene and lingering international resistance occasionally provided some hope for the possibility of establishing an independent, liberal Hun-

gary, but in 1867, after both sides had made concessions, a compromise was drafted which resulted in the Austro–Hungarian Monarchy. Although failing to ensure the nation's independence, the Compromise preserved Hungary's territorial integrity and gave some leeway for autonomy in the realm of domestic policy.

Kossuth remained a staunch opponent of the Compromise until his death in exile in 1894 at Torino, and although he had been powerless to alter the situation, his steadfast adherence to the cause of an independent, democratic Hungary is, in itself, representative of the nation's eternal fighting spirit —a spirit which in Kossuth's lifetime and at the time of the building of the Millennial Monument—had already become a model to emulate for generations to come.